Tolerating terrorism in the west

Has terrorism lost the power to shock and appal? Have liberal democracies learned to tolerate terrorism? Using case studies of governments' and societies' responses to terrorism, this book shows how attitudes towards terrorism have developed. Five western countries with differing political structures and histories are studied: Belgium, the Federal Republic of Germany, Israel, Italy and Spain. Each contributor examines the complex relationship between terrorism, society and government, and explores a plurality of attitudes and reactions, ranging from support through indifference to resistance. The analysis investigates the roles of social, political, legal, professional and religious institutions and movements in formulating the approved attitude towards terrorism that governs political bodies as well as society at large. The contributors come from a range of disciplines: Hans-Joseph Horchem was responsible for implementing the Federal Republic of Germany's anti-terrorist policy; Peter Waldmann is a sociologist; Francesco Sidoti is a historian; and Simon Petermann and Noemi Gal-Or are political scientists.

The editor, Noemi Gal-Or, is teaching at the Simon Fraser University, Canada. She received her PhD from the Institut Universitaire de Hautes Etudes Internationales, Geneva, and has published several books and articles on terrorism. She is the recipient of the Commission of the European Communities 1989–90 award for research into European integration.

Tolerating terrorism in the west

An international survey

Edited by
Noemi Gal-Or

London and New York

First published 1991
by Routledge
11 New Fetter Lane, London EC4P 4EE

Simultaneously published in the USA and Canada
by Routledge
a division of Routledge, Chapman and Hall, Inc.
29 West 35th Street, New York, NY 10001

Typeset by Selectmove Ltd, London
Printed and bound in Great Britain by
Biddles Ltd, Guildford and King's Lynn

British Library Cataloguing in Publication Data
Tolerating terrorism in the West : an international survey.
  1. Terrorism
  I. Gal-Or, Noemi
  305.625

  ISBN 0-415-02441-2

Library of Congress Cataloging in Publication Data
Tolerating terrorism in the West : an international survey / edited
  by Noemi Gal-Or.
      p.   cm.
  Includes bibliographical references and index.
    1. Terrorism--Europe--Public opinion. 2. Terrorism--Israel--Public
opinion. 3. Terrorism--Government policy--Europe. 4. Terrorism-
-Government policy--Israel. 5. Public opinion--Europe. 6. Public
opinion--Israel. I. Gal-Or, Noemi.
HV6433.E85T65 1991
363.3'2'094--dc20   91-3399
                                                              CIP

To Hans (Gideon)
for his help

Contents

Acknowledgments

I would like to express my gratitude to the Leonard Davis Institute for International Relations at the Hebrew University of Jerusalem for assisting this project with a research grant. Also, many thanks to my father in law, Gideon Gal-Or, who helped in the translation from German into English, which was necessitated by the international character of this enterprise. Brigid Bell deserves my appreciation for her outstanding editing of the manuscript, the chapters of which were all written by non-Anglophones.

Abbreviations

AD	Action Directe (Direct Action)
AI	Amnesty International
CCC	Cellules Communistes Combattantes (Communist Combat Cells)
CDU	Christian Democratic Union
CVP	Christelijke Volkspartji (Christian People's Party)
DFLP	Democratic Front for the Liberation of Palestine
EE	Euskadiko Ezquerra
ETA	Euzkadi ta Askatsuna (Basque Nation and Liberty)
FRAP	Revolutionary Front for Proletarian Action
GAL	Groupos Antiterroristas de Liberación
ICRC	International Committee of the Red Cross
IRA	Irish Republican Army
IZL	Irgun Tswai Leumi (Military National Organization)
LAOR	Lema'an Echai Vereai ('For my brothers and friends')
LEHI	Lohamei Herut Israel (Israel Freedom Fighters)
MKI	Israeli Communist Party
NPD	Nationalistische Partei Deutschland (German Nationalist Party)
PFLP	Popular Front for the Liberation of Palestine
PFLP-GC	Popular Front for the Liberation of Palestine–General Command
PLA	Palestinian Liberation Army
PLO	Palestinian Liberation Organization
PNV	Partido Nacional Vasco (Basque National Party)
PRL	Parti Reformateur Liberal (Liberal Reform Party)
PSOE	Partido Socialista de España (Spanish Socialist Party)

RAF	Rote Armee Fraktion (Red Army)
RKH	New Communist List
SPD	Sozialistische Partei Deutschland (German Socialist Party)
TNT	Terror Neged Terror (Terror anti Terror)

Introduction

Noemi Gal-Or

I

Terrorism has ceased to be an attraction. Political terrorism inflicted upon the international community, in particular terrorism in the western hemisphere since the late 1960s, has indeed become a routine ingredient of life in these societies. Initially, western societies were shocked by the rise of terrorism, a reaction which in the case of domestic terrorism has often been also transformed into indignation. Particularly in the young and vulnerable post-war democracies of the Federal Republic of Germany and Italy, governments were expected by the public to eradicate the problem once and for all. Yet, sharing with their people the burden and the memories of the not-so-distant outcomes of anarchy and terrorism and the consequent terrible slide into totalitarianism, these governments first reacted in confusion. Moreover, as if the challenge of domestic terrorism (the Red Army Faction in Germany or the Red Brigades in Italy) was not enough, these European target states were also soon forced to familiarize themselves with international terrorism, mainly originating in the Arab–Israeli conflict in the Middle East.

For the UK, targeted by terrorists also, this was not a new encounter. There already existed a measure of mental preparedness, even institutional experience in dealing with 'low intensity' warfare or with political violence: not only in Ireland, but also in the overseas colonies.

The revival of modern terrorism in the Basque region of Spain occurred at a time when Spain was still ruled by the dictator, Franco, and this explains the unbending attitude to terrorism.

France and Belgium were late comers to the European 'club' of states to be targeted by terrorism. Consequently, the process of reaction exemplified by Germany and Italy has served, to a certain extent, as a learning model for terrorism-affected neighbours.

Recovering from their initial surprise and impotence, both the German and Italian governments developed their own, differing, approaches to tackle the challenge of terrorism. The legislature, the executive 'coercive' bodies of the state (the police, the military and the intelligence services) have been all mobilized to counter this threat to democracy. Obviously though, the increasing sophistication of terrorism and its almost always international character have ruled out the possibility of isolating the treatment of terrorism to the confines of each individual state. Developments on the terrorist scene since the mid-1970s have dragged an increasing number of actors into the web.

To be sure, the process towards European integration – co-operation within the framework of the Common Market and, even more significantly the achievements within the Council of Europe and the active engagement of the European Parliament – have all contributed to the creation of a climate favourable to the collective brain-storming necessary to work out a joint attitude towards terrorism. But although integration is reassuring for the member states, it has been far more beneficial to the terrorists themselves. The more European democracies have become functionally and structurally integrated, the more terrorism has moved from purely domestic to international political violence. Moreover, terrorists did not content themselves with the tactical aspects of operating on the international (mostly regional) level. They have all too often switched from nationally defined goals to collective anti-western and anti-European terrorism too (for example German terrorists have ceased to focus exclusively on targets representing German politics, but target NATO or the multinational corporations as well). Non-European terrorists, mainly from the Middle East, are also attracted to this extremely vulnerable environment.

As a matter of fact, in ways reminiscent of their struggle to find the proper remedy against the growing rates of drug abuse, structural conditions in the western democracies have accommodated, though perhaps involuntarily, to terrorism. To be sure, in resisting terrorism, western democracies have undergone a thorough process of trial and error. Due to the internationalization of terrorism, Europeans could ignore neither Israel in counter-terrorist matters, nor the superpower

USA, which has inevitably become a partner in the western terrorist experience. This started with complications in Latin America and was followed by its drowning in the Middle-Eastern terrorist quicksands. Nevertheless, 'diplomatization' of the early and still very terrorist PLO and the reassessment of the policy of international co-operation with Iran or Syria were important decisions on the road towards disarming the terrorist threat. Significant, therefore, are developments such as the late birth of Belgian terrorism and the activity of the French terrorists which has continued despite these lessons, as well as the experience of Italy, where the commercialization of terrorism has resulted from the recognition of the profitable combination of political violence and drug trafficking.

II

Although constantly altering its appearances, modern terrorism is a permanent ingredient of modern political behaviour, not a temporary episode. Hence one of the more interesting concerns of the social scientist should be to study the effect terrorism has on society.

A long acquaintance with the literature on terrorism reveals that scholars have concentrated mainly on three major aspects: the phenomenon of terrorism, biographies and studies of terrorist actors and the organized governmental response to terrorism. To be sure, 'terrorist' literature has flourished like mushrooms after rain. To begin with, there is such an abundance of material that topic-oriented selection is indeed a difficult task to accomplish. Unfortunately, this is further complicated by the fact that a large number of publications which convey the pretention of scholarship are, however, too often cosmetically improved journalism.[1] In this age of sophisticated communication technology, computers enable the fast production and supply of information in response to customer's demand. This is indeed, the state of the art with respect to terrorism literature. Thus, stories like those about the famous but mysterious 'Carlos' (who, it seems, after all did not remain too long on the terrorist scene) are best sellers. The Palestinian Abu-Nidal figures no less prominently on the list of such best sellers, as do the legendary Ulrike Meinhof (RAF) or Mara Cagol (Red Brigades). And when gossipy curiosity is satisfied, readers may still indulge their interest in terrorism by reading into the various organizations practising terrorism, such as the different member organizations of the PLO or, more up-to-date and exotic, the mysteries and atrocities of the Peruvian Shining Path (Sendero Luminoso).

This is not to say that scientifically valid and responsible literature on terrorism does not exist. On the contrary it does, and has been respected for its contribution to our knowledge and understanding of the motivations of modern terrorism and the modes of organization and operation and, hence, to an improved and clearer insight into the phenomenon of terrorism at large.

The phenomenon of terrorism in general has been extensively discussed from its moral and ethical aspects. The incompatibility of terrorism as a mode of political behaviour with the norms and values of modern democratic societies, the role of terrorism within young developing ex-colonialist systems, and terrorism's role as a tool to alleviate political oppression, have been the topics to attract the expert's interest.

Further examination of the literature reveals that scholars from various disciplines have expressed great interest in researching the phenomenon of terrorism. Legal experts are perhaps under the greatest pressure to clarify our understanding of terrorism. Recurrent efforts to define terrorism and to distinguish the concept from other, often interfering, 'grey' terms, have usually assisted governments in their counter-terrorist policy.

Psychologists, socio-psychologists and criminologists are preoccupied with deciphering the 'terrorist mind', while political scientists, sociologists and historians point to the various circumstances for the revival of terrorism and call our attention to the socio-political and economic processes favouring the recourse to terrorist activity.

The variety of governmental responses to terrorism has also been abundantly reviewed. It ranges from the study of the role of the police, army and intelligence forces in countering domestic terrorism, to the survey of bilateral, regional and global efforts or omissions in the pursuance of this goal.[2] Governments as well as international organizations come under the magnifying glass of the experts, to such an extent that some governmental tactics, like covert action for instance, may already be considered as synonymous with terrorism itself. Past, unquestioning trust placed in the chosen representatives of the public has started to erode as there is an increase in suspicions concerning the sincerity of governmental intentions and the purity of tactics applied to counter terrorism.

Still, very little research, if any, has been done concerning the impact of terrorism on the western liberal democratic societies.

Citizens' confidence in their government is only one aspect of this subject. Inquiry, indeed, should encompass the broader spectrum of socio-political dynamics: the impact terrorism has had on western post-war morals and ethics generally as well as the compatibility between its scale of value preferences and the actual behaviour when responding to the terrorist challenge.

Terrorism was a shocking experience in the mid to late 1960s. It was sensed as appalling. Is this still the case today? Is terrorism still perceived as the unacceptable evil of so-called 'violence against innocents'? Is the intransigent exclusion of terrorism from among the 'rules of the game' still prevailing? And, if the perception of terrorism has indeed changed, what were the processes leading to the change and what are the outcomes? Or, was the moral dictum against terrorism, after all, only lip service, paid to cover a different reality? Who then, has participated in spreading the fog? What role does rhetoric, the application of certain linguistic terms, play in the social and political alteration of the concept 'terrorism'? What social and political functions do the values related to terrorism fulfil?

The list of questions is long and the scientific community has not yet boarded this ship of enquiry. True, some isolated attempts to discuss various aspects of this issue have been sporadically undertaken in the literature (in particular, the linguistic/rhetoric and theatre role of 'terrorism' in society).[3] Yet, there is no comprehensive discussion of the real (not speculative theoretical) socio-political effects of terrorism on society. Terrorism as an independent variable with its side-effects on society (rather than as a system-dependent variable, or its effectiveness in achieving its declared short to middle-term objectives or as a tool of governmental foreign policy) has not yet been studied. Furthermore, a comparative study addressing the effect of terrorism on a number of societies has not taken place either. This, indeed, will be the ambitious goal of the present volume.

III

Our project of studying the level of tolerance of terrorism in western societies has stretched over a number of years. We started the study in 1987 and therefore, acknowledge some limitations as to the freshness of the informative data. This, however, bears no effect on the content of our conclusions. Since we are dealing with socio-political trends and processes and not with the statics of terrorist assaults and governmental responses (important as these may be) we are confident that our general descriptions and analysis, as well as our theoretical conclusions, will stand the test of time.[4]

Ideas, particularly research topics, do not surprise us like UFOs suddenly arriving from outer space. My concern with the tolerance of terrorism in western society originated in a slowly ripening political and academic reaction to the social and political occurrences in my country, Israel. The shortcomings of the literature on terrorism, where I looked for answers to explain the modifications and inconsistencies in the attitude towards terrorism, and my own observations contributed to my decision to embark on the research into this political minefield.

I have recently completed a study of the so-called 'Jewish Underground', a Jewish-Israeli terrorist organization operating in Israel and the Territories from 1980 to 1984 (the year it was disbanded).[5] Events in Israel have evolved in such a way that although some members of the group were convicted and severely punished, they have enjoyed widespread popularity and an extremely well organized lobby has been trying to influence both judiciary and legislature, pleading for amnesty for the terrorists. Already acquainted with similar agitation in western European countries, this led me to consider the launching of an international comparative research project dealing with 'pro-terrorist lobbies' in the west. Western democratic states such as Italy, Spain, the Federal Republic of Germany, Belgium and Israel seemed a fairly representative selection for a number of reasons. Indeed, this 'mixture' of case studies lets us gain insight into a variety of combinations of types of terrorism and reactions to it.

The Federal Republic of Germany and Italy have experienced both left-and right-wing terrorism. In addition, terrorism there has become entangled in the Middle-Eastern terrorist scene as well. This provides the link with Israel, the primary concern of which has been Middle-Eastern terrorism, but which has been forced to face European terrorism too. On the other hand, Middle-Eastern state-sponsored terrorism became an experience shared by all societies studied here. Notwithstanding, international terrorism evolved also into the European/western/ capitalist/imperialist dimension, providing for the relevance of the otherwise different example of Belgium, a country with relatively little terrorist experience drawn into the turbulence already familiar in the Federal Republic of Germany and Italy. Though Spain merits inclusion as an example in its own right (a democracy evolving out of years of experience with dictatorship), it has become a relevant case study in this project precisely because it shares the same political system as the other cases studied. Besides these particularities, Spain and Israel are alike in having to tackle the problem of terrorism motivated by nationalist aspirations. Their experience in this domain might well coincide with equivalences drawn from Italy's troubles in South-Tyrol.

All the contributors were given the same questions to refer to in their studies. The focus of the analysis was laid on the support/indifference/resistance to terrorism (not an analysis of the terrorist groups themselves); on the level of voluntary social organization; formal social, political and professional institutions (political parties, leagues of human rights, etc.); the legislature and judiciary and the religious establishment too. However, the outcome of the different case studies depended upon the specific nature of each case.

In chapter 1, Peter Waldmann portrays a society torn between nationalist allegiance to the Basque ideal and the promises for a freer, democratic life within the framework of the multi-ethnic state. While inclination towards co-operation with the state has been on the rise, strong support for the terrorists, who struggle to separate the Basque region from Spain, has continued to persist. Nevertheless, support for terrorist behaviour as a legitimate method to achieve the separatist goal has diminished compared to the consistent support for the idea of separation itself.

Hans Joseph Horchem's chapter then focuses on the 'pockets' of support for terrorism within German society. Specific sectors of society, in particular the left-wing German terrorists, have for a while benefited from popular 'admiration'. At first capable of attracting wide support in the public at large, the increasing violence of the terrorists has drastically reduced popular support. Interestingly, both government and the public have been less alarmed by right-wing terrorism, which seems to have been played down as less threatening.

In chapter 3, the incremental change from absolute rejection of terrorism of all colours, to the slow acceptance of terrorism within the Jewish-nationalist vocation is traced. For the first time (almost since the establishment of the state of Israel) society and government have been faced with a situation in which the communal conflict between Israeli Jews and Palestinians is bursting out in terrorism and counter-terrorism. The consequences of this change and its effects on the attitude towards terrorism are the subjects discussed here.

The fourth chapter, by Simon Petermann, illustrates selectivity and, above all, calm in the public's response to terrorism even in a society which is only seldom afflicted by terrorism.

Chapter 5 provides us with a thorough insight into the labyrinth of Italian society and politics. Terrorism in Italy derives from various sources and has enjoyed varying degrees and forms of institutional and privately organized support, respectively. Francesco Sidoti makes it clear that, after all and in certain circumstances, terrorism is not among the worst enemies of the polity and society. It might all the same be an efficient political and economic instrument, even when it happens to be applied within the framework of a democratic regime.

Finally, the concluding chapter addresses the data analysed in each of the case studies. Comparing the different situations and conditions, we are nevertheless, able to draw some general conclusions pertinent to the way societies and their representatives in democratic regimes prefer to approach terrorism. By researching into the broader framework of the attitude to terrorism in society at large (not the moral dilemma and operational concerns only) we intended to make a breakthrough for the study of this 'niche' within the field of terrorism studies. This should, we hope, be followed by additional comparative studies and more case studies to complement and perfect our preliminary effort.

NOTES

1   See Wardlaw, Grant, 'Terror as an Instrument of Foreign Policy', Inside Terrorist Organizations, ed. David C. Rapoport, London: Frank Cass, 1988, pp. 237–59.

2   Homer, Frederick D., 'Government Terror in the United States: An Exploration of Containment Policy', The State as Terrorist, eds. Michael Stohl and George A. Lopez, Westport, Greenwood Press, 1984, pp. 167–81; Chomsky, Noam, The Culture of Terrorism, Boston: South End Press, 1988.

3   Hocking, Jenny, 'Orthodox Theories of "Terrorism": The Power of Politicised Terminology', Politics, 19 (2), 1984, pp. 103–11; Rada, S.E., 'Trans-national Terrorism as Public Relations?', Public Relations, 11(3), 1985, pp. 26–33.

4   The current (1990) hostage release affairs in Lebanon involving extensive international diplomatic agitation from the USA, UK, Syria, Iran, Israel and others is another up-to-date example.

5   Gal-Or, Noemi, The 'Jewish Underground': Our Terrorism, Tel Aviv: Hakibbutz Hameuchad, Kav Adom Series, 1990. All the Hebrew references hereafter have been translated into English.

Chapter 1

From the vindication of honour to blackmail: the impact of the changing role of ETA on society and politics in the Basque region of Spain

Peter Waldmann

In order to appraise correctly the importance of ETA and the kind of terrorism it has been practising inside and outside the Basque region, one should first differentiate this type of ethnically motivated use of violence from the terrorism of radicalized groups of the middle class in such highly industrialized countries as the Federal Republic of Germany, France and Italy, which is energized by a revolutionary social ideology. While the numerous outrages of the RAF and the 'Action Directe', both enjoying an extremely limited membership, meet with a lack of understanding or even disgust on the part of their respective societies, ETA may rely on the sympathy and indirect or even direct support of a considerable segment of the Basque population (the same may be said with regard to the IRA). In the era of the Franco dictatorship, until 1975, practically the entire Basque population backed the terror organization; its members, the Etarras, were considered heroes and martyrs who were upholding the honour of a culturally and politically tyrannized people. Since the transformation of Spain's government into a parliamentary monarchy this silent consensus has broken down as many Basques are no longer able to understand the sense of bloody outrages in a political system seeking to grant other, peaceful means for safeguarding interests. However, a minority within the ethnic majority continues to stand solidly behind the terrorist organization. Due to its political engagement, its methods of enforcement and last but not least to the lasting irresoluteness of the remaining political forces in the Basque region, this minority, the left nationalists (abertzales), exercises an influence in the region greatly exceeding its numerical significance.

This influence will be reflected in an opening section summarizing the history of the nationalist movement and, within this context, the significance of ETA. Another section will deal with the forces and working mechanisms, in and by which the power of ETA and its adherents is manifested. Finally, the third section will consider the political initiatives and measures taken by the Spanish government to counter the influence of ETA and to break up the pact of solidarity between the terror organization and the Basque people.

THE HISTORICAL CONTEXT: ETA AS VINDICATOR OF THE HONOUR OF THE BASQUE PEOPLE

Simply stated, we can discern two main phases of the nationalist awakening of the Basque population, which for centuries stood at the fringe of the political events in Spain. The first phase comprised the last decades of the nineteenth century; the second one started in the 1960s under the Franco dictatorship. The first phase, closely connected with the name of the founder and charismatic leader of the movement, Sabino Arana y Goiri, has quite recently and repeatedly been the subject of extensive historiographic research, providing us with reliable and thorough information.[1] Therefore, it may be taken for granted that the principal group bearing the then new trend was recruited from within the Basque middle classes. They saw their economic and social position endangered by the development of a Basque grand bourgeoisie, which in those decades pursued the building up of heavy industry and powerful banks in the area of Bilbao (Vizcaya). Sabino Arana y Goiri's alarming prophecy that industrialization and urbanization, inevitably accompanied by secularization, would jeopardize ethnic individuality and solidarity, found an echo principally among traditionalist sections of the population in the provinces and among those primary producers such as peasants, tenant farmers and fishermen, who identified with Basque folklore and the Basque language – the Euskara. They were just a minority of the regional population, which caused the nationalist movement for a long time to operate from a position of weakness. This, however, gave it a particularly bitter and aggressive trait. The resentment and contempt of the nationalists were primarily aimed at the numerous Spanish workers who flowed into Vizcaya from neighbouring provinces, attracted by the job supply and the relatively high wages in the new industrial area. They were considered to be a racially inferior foreign body, threatening the bond and traditional consensus of values of the population. The Partido Nacional Vasco (PNV), for decades maintaining a political monopoly within the nationalist camp, assumed the political representation of the movement.

The structural conditions at the outset of the second phase of national mobilization, which began in the 1960s and is still going on, were similar to those in the nineteenth century. While the Spanish economy suffered a severe setback as a result of the civil war (1936–9) and the course of economic autarchy initially adopted by Franco, a gradual recovery began in the mid-1950s. The role of pace setter of the reactivated industrialization, which rapidly expanded in the 1960s and early 1970s, was again taken on by Catalonia and the Basque region, the two traditional industrial districts of Spain.[2] While in the nineteenth century the industrial boom inside the Basque region was limited mainly to Bilbao, it now covered the two coastal provinces Vizcaya and Guipuzcoa, particularly gaining ground in the narrow valleys of the hinterland of these two provinces. The percentage of those working in the primary occupations decreased to less than 10 per cent of the total numbers of employed. As in the first industrial push, the Basque style of life had difficulties in surviving under the changed conditions of a modern industrial society, since it was deeply rooted in a rural provincial environment. But it was a political factor which threatened the Basque culture even more than the modernization process: namely the aim of the Franco regime to establish a unitary state.

General Franco believed that the appropriate moment had come once and for all, to break, the backbone of the nationalist movement which had been gaining strength along the northern periphery of the country since the beginning of the century and was threatening the unity of the state. Now was the time to weld the Spaniards from above into a homogeneous nation. During the civil war the Basques as well as the Catalonians had fought alongside the Republicans against the rebels; after the victory they had to pay heavily for this. Immediately after the capture and subjugation of both regions (the Basque region 1937, Catalonia 1939), repression began, aimed first and foremost at suppressing any manifestation of cultural autonomy. Hundreds were executed, thousands were imprisoned and hundreds of thousands fled into exile. Public administration was purged and all the local officials were replaced by functionaries from other parts of Spain. All the testimonies of regional culture were removed, destroyed and forbidden. Books and periodicals in the regional language disappeared from the libraries and bookshops; institutes and academies dedicated to the preservation and research of regional tradition were closed down; regional monuments were demolished and the names of streets and businesses were translated into Castilian. The use of the Catalonian and Basque languages by authorities or in the public services was punished and the regional language and culture consequently banished from education. Teaching in schools was taken over by teachers from other parts of the country; children were not even allowed to communicate with one another in their mother tongue. In other words, the regime left no stone unturned in its efforts to exterminate regional cultures and to crush any instance of nationalist resistance. How did the minority population react to this threat to its existence?

The resistance and the will to survive mainly manifested themselves in three ways.[3] The first way was to boycott a regime which ignored them as an ethnic entity. Plebiscites on important political issues organized by the dictator and held at long intervals – 1947, 1966 and 1976 (the latter took place after Franco's death but it belongs to the Franco era in the wider sense) – were occasions to demonstrate an attitude of political denial. Especially in the two plebiscites of 1966 and 1976 the number of abstentions was higher in the Basque region than in any Spanish district. Another strategy for survival was the retreat from the state into civilian society. Basque society comprises a rich variety of groups and associations, to which the principal bearers of ethnic folklore belong. Important in this context are friendship groups of youths (*quadrilla*), boy scouts, mountaineers' and ramblers' associations, sport clubs, choirs and folklore groups as well as gastronomic societies. Notwithstanding the rigorous exercise of power by the Franco regime, it could not, penetrate these social groupings to break through the hermetic seal of silence which served the minority to protect itself against the external pressure of the regime. A secret code among the members of the minorities came into being, which gave even apparently harmless gestures and ways of conduct a definite meaning of protest, such as the participation in a reading circle or the visit to a theatre performance or sports event. While the two forms of resistance described above bore a primarily passive character, the third one was equal to the challenge of the dictatorship. It started with attacks on symbols and installations of the central government and later degenerated into assassination of policemen and representatives of the regime. The originators were members of the secret organization ETA.

There is not enough room here to elaborate on the internal and external development of ETA as well as on its role in the regional resistance against the Franco regime. We shall therefore limit ourselves to outlining a few points which we ought to be aware of in order to evaluate properly the great prestige which the terrorists enjoyed among parts of the Basque population.[4]

ETA, officially founded in the late 1950s after a prolonged previous history, emerged as a result of the initiative of a group of students, who in the beginning mainly devoted themselves to the study of the Basque language and literature. Their radicalization should in the first place be attributed to two facts: the severe persecution exercised by the Spanish security authorities and suppression of any manifestation of the desire for ethnic cultural survival (for example the singing of Basque songs) and the insignificant presence of the moderate PNV in the Basque region, whose leadership in Paris rejected violent resistance, preferring instead to await the end of the Franco tyranny.

After having turned to the course of violence in the 1960s, ETA persisted in sticking to it. Indeed the matter of whether it would not be advisable to renounce terrorism for the sake of a political opening was frequently discussed in the executive committees; also the Marxist wing, strong at that time, asserted that the prosecution raids of the state, provoked by the assaults were impeding the mobilization of the labour force. But in the end the representatives of the 'hard' wing always gained the upper hand after presenting bloodshed and kidnapping as *faits accomplis*. Groups disagreeing with this new course were either expelled from the organizations or left voluntarily, founding new organizations and parties.

The Basques in general were particularly impressed by the courage and the determination with which the Etarras engaged in an apparently hopeless struggle. In this sense, significance should be attached to their attitude with regard to the Burgos Trial in 1970, which also aroused considerable international interest. Though the regime had staged it as a show trial against rebellious traitors, the accused ETA members, who fearlessly pleaded their cause and even sang the Basque national anthem in the court room, turned it into a tribunal of indictment against the dictatorship. From that moment on, the young terrorist organization has not been faced with any more recruiting problems. In particular, youths living in the hinterland of the province of Guipuzcoa were eager to join it. ETA members moved in Basque society like 'fish in water' (Mao Tse Tung, *Theorie des Guerillakriegs oder Strategie der Dritten Welt*, 1970, Hamburg).

In retrospect, giving public expression to the determination of ethnic survival has been the main achievement of ETA.[5] By its assaults it proved the vulnerability of the dictatorship and at the same time upheld the honour and self-esteem of the minority which otherwise was compelled to endure the oppression silently. The Basques will always bear this in mind. Thanks to ETA, the resoluteness of opposition by the Basque people, evident from the numerous demonstrations and strikes since 1970, has gained renewed strength and eloquence. Between 1970 and 1975 no less than four strikes took place in the country of the Basques, paralysing public life.

Political sensitization and intensive mobilization of the Basque population caused by the dictatorship manifested themselves in these general strikes, which did not subside even after Franco's death. The indignation of the Basque population at the wrong they had suffered was too great and their subsequent rejection of the centralism emanating from Madrid was so strong that it threatened their relationship with the democratic regime which succeeded Franco's dictatorship. Only a clear breach with the Franquist government system by the new democratic leadership elite could have prevented this transference effect. As we know, such a breach has not taken place – neither generally nor with regard to the attitude of the central authorities towards the Basque minority. The Basques imprisoned during the Franco era were only gradually set free and only after exertion of pressure. The Spanish security forces continued to use a strong hand at demonstrations in the region of Cantabria. The constitutional recognition of the right of self-government of this small people took several years in coming (not until 1979). No wonder that the general strikes continued under these circumstances and that ETA's assertion, that violence was an inevitable expedient to pressure the centralist politicians into reasonability, was widely accepted.

The growing dissociation of large groups of the population from the terrorist organization set in only as late as the 1980s. The reasons are the obvious brutality and inhumanity of the current ETA actions on the one hand, which compared to the assaults in the Franco era, no longer imply any sort of risk of government persecution to the terrorists, and, on the other hand, fundamental changes in the political context compared with that era which make the violent enforcement of political aims seem illegitimate as well as less promising. But there are three points which should not be overlooked. First, the rational rejection of the course of violence should not be identified with any emotional renunciation of the bond with the terrorist organization, since the after-effect of the historical indebtedness is still strongly felt. Second, the discord primarily relates to the use of violence as a political tool. With regard to its political aim, namely to obtain from the central government a more comprehensive independence than that granted by the law of self-government passed in 1979, ETA may, however, rely on the support of over a third of the Basque population. Third, and in conclusion, ETA has succeeded in building up a social and political network dissociated from its terror activities, which represents and emphasizes its political aspirations and ideas.

It will be necessary to analyse some of the representative groups and methods of enforcement of this network, which, is so to speak, the civilian lobby of ETA. First, however, we will survey the political murders perpetrated by ETA (figure 1.1) and examine the attitude of the Basque population towards central ethical problems, particularly with regard to the political future of ETA.

Market research published in *Cambio 16*, 18 July 1985, examined the attitude of the Basque population towards certain key problems, especially towards ETA and armed struggle:

1   How would you classify yourself in the following five groups?
    - I am a Spaniard only   8
    - more Spanish than Basque   5
    - Spanish as much as Basque   63
    - more Basque than Spanish   52
    - Basque only   32
    - no response   3

2   Which of the following political solutions for the Basque region do you prefer?
    - integration in a unitary state   5
    - autonomy according to the statute presently in force   45
    - autonomy tending towards complete independence   81
    - complete independence   71
    - no response   6

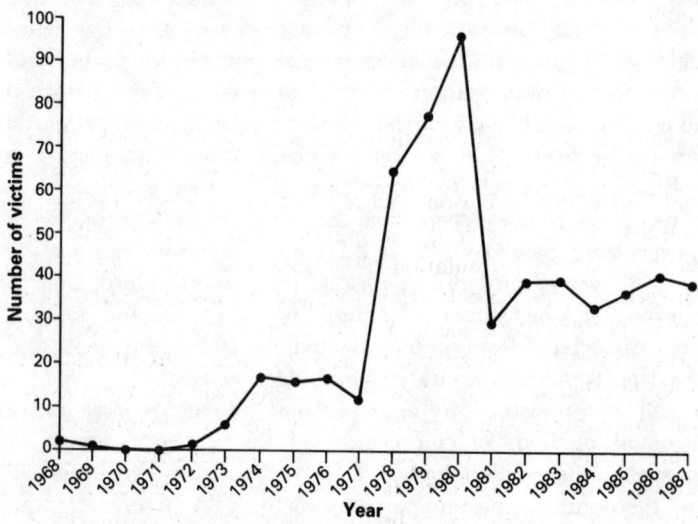

Figure 1.1   Victims of ETA terrorism*

Source: Documentation Centre of ABC
* Different sources draw slightly differing conclusions in respect of the number of ETA victims (for the period until 1980 compare R. P. Clark, 1984, p. 125). The graph does, however, aptly present the overall trend reflected in all the investigations.

3   With which statement about ETA do you agree?
   - It never had the right to exist   62
   - It had a right to exist in the past but it no longer does   54
   - It still has a right to exist   61
   - no response   31

4   Should Etarras giving up armed struggle be granted amnesty?
   - yes   7
   - no   71
   - no response   31

5   Should the ETA give up armed struggle and dissolve?
   - yes   67
   - no   31
   - no response   11

6 Should the government negotiate with the ETA?
    –   yes   36
    –   no   12
    –   no response   61

Since the end of the Franco dictatorship numerous polls on the ethnic problems and the question of the legitimacy of the use of violence in the Basque region have taken place, partly differing in their results, due not only to the differing times of the polls but also to the differing formulation of the questions. It is, however, an ever-recurring fact that 10–15 per cent of the Basque population support ETA (for details see R. P. Clark, 1984, page 166 onward). Concerning question 1: it should be borne in mind that 50 per cent of the population presently living in the region are descendants of Spanish immigrants. Though the first generation of descendants often endeavours to counter-balance its non-Basque origin by over-identification with its new homeland, many of the new immigrants nevertheless feel themselves to be Spaniards only or Spaniards as well as Basques.

THE CURRENT SITUATION IN ETA

Herri Batasuna (HB)

Two trends have characterized the development of the party system in the Basque region since the end of the Franco era.[6] On the one hand nationalist parties, active within the Basque region, are obviously gaining ground opposite the Spanish oriented ones. While the PNV at the time of the Second Republic (1931–6) received on average only a third of the votes alongside the strong all-Spanish parties, the number voting for Basque parties has meanwhile increased to almost two-thirds of the total voting population, and the result of this development cannot be foreseen. This, which would be the second trend, is largely dependent on the ideological and organizational distinction within the Basque party spectrum since the transition to the constitutional monarchy. Unlike the pre-Franco era, there presently also exist a Basque 'left wing' beside a Basque 'right wing'. The former is represented by two parties: Euskadiko Ezquerra (EE) and Herri Batasuna (HB), which have both originated from ETA splinters. But while

EE has gradually dissociated itself from the terror organization now to rank with its opponents and consequently pursuing a socialist party programme, HB is the most important lobby of ETA within the political sphere.

Actually HB is not a true party but an election alliance, consisting of numerous groups, small parties, committees and the like, headed by the Mesa Nacional (literally: National Table), a co-ordinating body numbering almost 50 members. Due to its strong orientation towards grass-roots democracy and to the great importance attached to the active engagement of its members, in some respects HB resembles a socio-political movement rather than a party in the conventional sense, and it is indeed a movement, which the 'Batasuneros' endeavour above all to carry into Basque politics and society. Principally opposed to the charter of autonomy and the division of responsibilities between the central state and the 'Autonomous Basque Community' (the official term) stipulated therein, HB strives in every possible way to prevent the normalization of the political situation in the Basque region. One of the means adopted is the systematic boycott of the parliamentary agencies. Though HB leaders run in the elections for the regional and national parliaments, they refuse, if elected, to occupy their parliamentary seats and to take part in the decision-making process (except at the level of the local councils, where they collaborate). Instead they stir up unrest whenever a suitable occasion presents itself. The flag dispute constitutes a good example. At the Basque festival every summer the question arises of which flags should be hoisted – the Spanish or the Basque flag, both or none. Year after year the HB has exploited the occasion of the festival to underline the right of the Basque region to complete independence by ostentatiously hauling down and burning the Spanish flag. This provocation has inevitably brought about the intervention of the security forces and severe, often bloody clashes between militant nationalists and politicians. HB welcomes these clashes, which underline the party's role as the promoter of resistance to the political status quo, mobilizing all the dissatisfied sections of the population and endeavouring to prove the inefficiency of the existing institutional order.

Its basic attitude of boycotting the parliamentary democracy draws HB very near to ETA, for the terror organization also maintains that, despite the transition to democracy, as a matter of fact there has been no change in the extent of suppression and incapacitation by Madrid. The Basques have been deprived of basic democratic freedoms and political dissidents in the region are imprisoned and tortured. The political representatives of the region have joined in the dirty game played by Madrid, thus betraying the genuine interests of the Basque people. ETA maintains that in order to achieve definite national freedom one must not embark on empty compromises but remain tough, going on with militant demonstrations and violent attacks. The conformity of objectives of HB and ETA is particularly evident in their common reference to the so-called 'Alternative KAS'. This is a five-point programme, originating in the 1970s, which specifies the minimum demands for giving up armed resistance. These demands read as follows[7]:

1   Granting of a general amnesty for ETA prisoners presently held in Spanish prisons, and the waiving of formal permission to return for the numerous Etarras who have escaped abroad, especially to France;
2   Granting of all the democratic rights of freedom, including the democratic right of self-determination;
3   Withdrawal of all Spanish security forces from the Basque region;
4   Improvement of the living conditions of the mass Basque population and the Basque working class in particular;
5   Inclusion of Navarra in the Autonomous Basque Community, following a plebiscite.

It would take too long to comment on these five points as well as to enumerate the reasons why the government in Madrid is reluctant or only conditionally ready to accept them. But it is important to consider the 'tactical' character of the five-point programme, the acceptance of which by the opposite side is meant to be a pre-condition of further negotiations. The strategic long-range objective of the radical nationalists is to achieve a total breaking away from the Spanish Federation of States, in order to realize the democratic right of self-determination of the Basque people.

The conformity of long-range and immediate objectives as well as the methods of enforcement invites the presumption that there exist additional ties between the ETA and HB. This presumption, based on sporadic evidence and indications, has continuously been reiterated in Spain. But as the representatives of HB have always accentuated their organizational independence and no pertinent information from ETA has been available, for a long time this continued to be mere speculation and suspicion. Only by the recent discovery of several ETA hiding places in southern France has the nature of the relationship between the two groups become more transparent. Thus the hypothesis of the existence of an extensive organizational, financial and personal co-ordination and even involvement has been confirmed.[8] Documents have been found which reveal that associations politically connected with HB have received financial contributions from ETA funds. Minutes of joint meetings show that ETA has exercised considerable influence on individual political decisions of the party and has had a momentous say in the appointment of personnel for establishment associated with the party. On the other hand, HB members have repeatedly assisted the terror organization in the construction of supply and arms depots and to escape in cases of emergency. It is no secret that retired, and sometimes even active, Etarras participate in the work of the party organization and at times play an important role. Well-known is the case of Carlos Yoldi, a 23-year-old member of ETA. During his detention he was included in the party ticket by HB and then, after his election as deputy, he was nominated by the same party for Basque prime minister.

Altogether, a subtle division of functions between the two organizations reveals itself, whereby ETA is the obvious superior of HB and makes the final decision in cases of doubt. ETA embodies the principles of a rigid hierarchy and discipline is a pre-condition for its underground activity, while HB stands for the opposite principle of an open, loose formation in the legal, political domain. The membership of the former is necessarily limited; the latter makes allowance for the demand of mobilization among large groups to serve the national cause. ETA tries to unhinge the parliamentary constitutional state by means of violent actions; HB pesters it by infiltrating and undermining its institutions. Finally, while ETA, due to its seclusion from the 'dirty' political routine, is making an important contribution to the upholding of national myths – the myth of Basque heroes and martyrs as well as of a future impeccable community – HB, on the other hand, protesting noisily, expresses the dissatisfaction of many Basques with actual current economic social and political hardships.

It can be easily proved that the division of labour outlined above is not the wishful programme of a radical intellectual system, but rather a functional system which in practice has frequently stood the test. The public campaigns and demonstrations usually staged by HB after ETA outrages in order to distract the Basque public and to convince it of the necessity of continuing the armed struggle may serve as an example, or the reaction of ETA to the denunciation of political adversaries by HB, which may come to a sentence of death for the person concerned. However, the good performance of HB in elections clearly proves the usefulness and success of the double strategy pursued by both organizations. Its portion of 15 per cent of all the votes cast in the Basque region has remained rather constant since 1979. In the recent elections to the regional parliament (at the end of 1986) it even rose to 17.5 per cent.[9] It appears that a considerable part of the Basque population does not resent the frank identification of the left-nationalist party coalition with the course of violence followed by ETA, but on the contrary supports it.

The reasons for this conduct will become clearer after looking more closely at the adherents of HB. As a matter of fact, it has become apparent that it enjoys the backing of the same social strata from which ETA is used to mobilizing its new blood.[10] The typical HB-sympathizer is 20 to 30 years old, comes from the province of Guipuzcoa, belongs to the lower middle class (for example, he may be a skilled worker or a junior clerk), has an intermediate education and feels himself primarily a Basque. The division of functions between the political set-up and the terror organization as described above should, following a precise analysis, be augmented to the functional triangle: ETA–HB–sympathizers whereby each group is fulfilling certain duties: ETA represents the military avant-garde of the struggle for national liberation and provides its leadership cadre. The mass of ETA followers and sympathizers constitutes the parent group of the terror organization, extending it its emotional and logistic support and, if necessary, complementing its personnel. Its support of HB, on the other hand, enables the movement to demonstrate its presence in the legal domain, in parliament and on the street. HB, for its part, avails itself of its functions as political representative and mobilizing agent, but at the same time serves as connecting link between the other two components of the movement, publicly voicing the latter's solidarity and ties.

The crystallization of this strange, partly legally and partly illegally operating protest front should be evaluated in the light of the increasing alienation of many adolescents and young people of the institutions of the parliamentary democracy, a phenomenon which is found in all the industrial countries, but is particularly perceptible in the Basque region. It should be noted within this context that in the referendum of 1978 the Spanish constitution did not receive a majority among the qualified Basque voters, and even the Autonomy Law gained but a small majority. This has caused E. Laraña to speak of the illegitimization of the principle of representation in the Basque region, affecting all the agencies of the parliamentary democracy.[11] The recurring achievements of HB in elections might after all be explained by the fact that it is this populist party which succeeded most in breaking through the political apathy of large sections of Basque voters resulting from the legitimacy issue. Indeed, HB is, according to Laraña, housing feelings and, due to its centralized structure and appeal to basic democratic principles, complying with the nostalgic wishes of many Basques for the re-establishment of small units of self-management. Furthermore, the HB leaders, Laraña continues, are embodying the traditional type of personalized, charismatic authority ties, still meeting with approval in the Basque region.

A network of militant social protest groups

Though HB, as the political exponent of the militant separatist movement, is standing in the foreground it is by no means standing alone. The political sensitization and mobilization of the Basque population, linked with the above-mentioned tendency towards association, has produced a multitude of associations, committees and groupings. In their subject matter or objectives they are all more or less directly concerned with the national suppression and its removal, and consequently also with ETA. It is significant to note that there is no disagreement between the antagonists and champions of the national movement with regard to the assumption that ETA and HB constitute the focus of a widely ramified network of radical nationalistic groups and societies. A recently published report by the Madrid police does not entirely contradict findings such as those of Lang, who observes the Basque secession movement with obvious sympathy.[12] In the following survey we shall try to give a rough idea of the expansion of this network and of its major modes of action.

Groupings

   Youth Organizations of HB (Jarrai)
   Nationalist Trade Unions (LAB)

Linguistic and Cultural Organizations (AEK)

Anti-Atomic Energy and Ecological Groups

Anti-NATO and Anti-Military committees

Committee supporting fugitive ETA members (Comité de apoyo a los refugiados)

Amnesty groups, advocating unconditional remission of punishment for imprisoned Etarras (Gestoras por Amnistia)

Radical Priests' Movement

Solidarity movement for Central America

Leftist, nationalist newspapers (for example the daily *EGIN* and the weekly *Punto y Hora*) and pirate radio

Modes of action

Rallies in public streets and squares, including speeches, singing, war-cries, etc. (sometimes degenerating into aggressive offences, such as the obstruction of traffic)

Boycotts (for example, against French goods)

Marches, bus tours, round trips, at times to distant destinations, for propaganda and solidarity purposes

Formation of human chains, human blocks, demonstrative self-confinement (for instance in churches)

Funeral and memorial services (on the occasion of the return of a killed Etarras to his home village or in order to commemorate dead or missing Etarras)

Sales and fund raising drives (for example to finance bus rides to distant prisons)

Scientific events: lectures, seminars, conferences, public debates

Cultural events, such as exhibitions, films, posters

Public relations campaigns through press conferences, advertising in left-nationalist newspapers, cable campaigns (to prisoners) and submission of petitions to authorities

Festivals (with speeches, banquets, music and dancing)

It would be wrong to suggest that all the associations enumerated above were directly steered by ETA or HB. Such a simplified view would not do justice to the complexity and internal plurality of the radical nationalist camp. Within HB there exist divergent wings; not all its leaders and sub-groups agree with the ETA course, nor do they yield to the dictate of the terror organization. The same applies to the other groupings, sometimes in an even more accentuated form.

It would be wrong, for example, to label the radical priests or the linguistic and cultural associations as instruments of ETA. The reality is, however, that they do not unequivocally and publicly dissociate themselves from the terrorists, but display understanding and forbearance for the continued assaults and perhaps even welcome them. This unites all these groups and may even justify to range them in the block of militant nationalism. Thus they contribute, willingly or not, to the perpetuation and further strengthening of the radical-nationalist movement, which confirms and legitimizes the ETA's avant garde claim in respect of the struggle for national independence. From the list of supporting groups we have picked out the Basque rock music scene and the amnesty organization, which are rather different from each other, in order to illustrate the ETA's mode of functioning.

A specific kind of Basque music, starting as early as the 1970s, has developed alongside the traditional forms of Basque music culture such as male choirs or the singing of improvised verses by individuals (bertsolari).[13] But only during the 1980s did the rock music of the region obtain its fast, hard and aggressive lineation and there emerged those well-known texts devised for the Basque situation, which music critics consider a unique phenomenon and call 'radical Basque rock'. In the meantime, rock interludes have become an integral part of every larger festival programme in the Basque region, frequently attracting thousands of young people.

One of the characteristics of the Basque rock songs is the mood of deep frustration which they spread and, directly related to this, the defiant attitude directed against the existing social and political system. Though the police, army and army service, politicians and religion are the top targets of the onslaught of the Basque rock musicians, nevertheless they spare nothing and nobody, not even the revolution and not even the Basque region. The background of the aggressive slogans and verses is partly the desperate economic situation of the young people in the district of Cantabria – the unemployment rate is distinctly higher than the Spanish average – which, together with their strong political consciousness, has driven many of them to a radical left attitude and has, among even a larger number, nourished anarchism, which finds its expression, for example, in the widespread abstention from elections.

The radical rock undeniably reflects accurately this furious 'anti-everything' (anti-todo) attitude of a substantial section of the Basque youth, and the tumultuous and at times chaotic rock festivals faithfully portray their world outlook and the opportunities of orientation and action seized in this world. For a long time the all-Spanish mass media have almost completely ignored the radical Basque rock, another reason for the adolescents of the region to identify with it.

It was the HB and other representatives of the left nationalist bloc who quite early became aware of the musical protest movement and its political potential. It is true that the preconditions for rapprochement were favourable, as the rock rebels shared with HB the rejection of the parliamentary system and its institution. From the outset the possibility could not be eliminated that HB would submit to the youngsters' judgement of parties and politics. But the militant left nationalists anticipated this possibility and took the initiative. The first large Basque rock festival, which became a striking success and helped the participating groups to gain great popularity, took place within the framework of an anti-NATO demonstration in Tudela (Navarra) in 1983, organized by the daily *EGIN*. Since then *EGIN* and HB have become the most ardent patrons of the Basque radical rock, which is understandable, as this new form of music has proved to be a most effective instrument of propaganda for left-nationalist ideas and slogans. The song lyrics, the general environment (where ETA was repeatedly cheered), the drives and exhibitions for the benefit of the prisoners – all these perfectly fit the political course pursued by the separatist party alliance. Indeed, some of the most popular rock groups originate directly from the youth organization. Not all the admirers of Basque rock songs are impressed by the political message brought forward by them. Nevertheless it certainly is remarkable how the left-nationalist party coalition succeeded in settling down in a specific domain of modern juvenile culture, skipping the generation hurdle and scoring a political socialization effect, which might have a considerable impact on the division of votes in future elections in the Basque region.

Our second illustration, concerning the amnesty movement (Gestoras por Amnistia), is closely connected with the aforementioned demand of the Alternative KAS for the unconditional release of all Basque prisoners and for the permission for all those escaped abroad to return without the usual formalities. Notwithstanding the amnesty granted in 1977 to many Etarras imprisoned during the Franco era, there are still some 400 ETA members imprisoned in Spanish jails and about 1,000 Etarras are thought to be fugitives seeking asylum in other countries. These are our current figures, but the delicate question of the imprisonment problem, touching deep wounds of the Basques, unfolds only in respect to the recent history. It is commonly known that the Basques had to bear the brunt of the Franquist suppression. One author has calculated that in 1975 the political prisoners from Euskadi made up 70 per cent of all the sentences meted out in Spain. If the years of their imprisonment were divided among the entire Basque population, thirteen hours of detention would fall upon each inhabitant.[14] The transition to democracy has not brought about any fundamental change in this regard. According to periodically published announcements by *EGIN*, approximately 11,000 Basques are supposed to have been arrested since 1975 as a result of the application of the anti-terror laws, of whom three were tortured to death and another three disappeared. Taking into account the limited size of the population living in the Basque region (slightly over 2.5 million) and also that certain groups of the population were more intensively exposed to the persecution by the security authorities than others, it is easy to understand the existence of some kind of repression trauma among the former groups. Particularly in some areas of the hinterland of the province of Guipuzcoa there is no village or quarter, no large family or circle of friends not mourning the loss of someone through death, flight or detention. Here the Gestoras por Amnistia enjoy particularly strong support and they may rely on their appeals to meet with a consistent response.

The Gestoras have built up a well organized body headed by a national committee, whose dynamics are, however, in the main determined by an actively engaged membership,[15] a trait shared with other left-nationalist groupings. This engagement centres around the economic, legal and emotional care for the detainees as well as, in general, the denunciation of violations of human rights and severe detention conditions. Fulfilling the tasks as outlined is by no means easy, as the majority of the ETA members are detained in central or southern Spain, far away from the Basque region. The organization of periodical parcel dispatches and of personal contacts, at times including solidarity visits by larger groups,[16] involves considerable pecuniary and time-consuming preparation. Communication does not at all run along a one-way track from the relatives, acquaintances and supporters to the detainees, but on the contrary the terrorists themselves let their voices be heard regularly. For instance, they demanded an explanation from the

HB delegate to the Council of Europe for a critical comment of his on an attempted ETA action. It would impair the scope of the amnesty groups to limit their action to the individual assistance extended to the prisoners from humanitarian motives. They maintain uninterrupted contact between the prisoners and the radical nationalist bloc, thus ensuring that the militancy of the detained Etarras continues to be an asset for the movement. At the same time they prevent the prisoners from evading the control of the movement, and finally they keep alive the binding memory of common sacrifices and deprivations for the sake of the national cause among both the detained Etarras and their radical parent groups in the Basque region.

This integrating and co-ordinating function of the Gestoras was very much in evidence during 1987, as the Spanish government intensified its efforts to break the solidarity of ETA prisoners. On the one hand the detention conditions were aggravated; Basque detainees in particular, until then kept away from other criminals, were dispersed in small groups among numerous Spanish prisons and there put in solitary confinement. On the other hand, the government renewed its offer of individual remission of punishment, provided the individual terrorist renounced the future use of violence. It is above all this latter initiative which was vehemently attacked by the left-nationalist circles. They justly regarded it as an attempt to disrupt the collectivity of the detained terrorists from within and to break their spirit of resistance. Both the detainees' groups and the representatives of the amnesty organizations speak of an attempted extortion on the part of the Madrid central authorities, who were attempting to extract a confession of repentance from the prisoners whom they hold as hostages, in order to weaken the national resistance front. The temptation of each prisoner to save his or her own skin would be detrimental to the whole movement and to the fate of all prisoners. Hence, solidarity and pressure on the government as a group is preferable for the sake of both individual and collective interests. The only acceptable solution would be the unconditional release of all the Basque prisoners.

In order to gain the maximum publicity the tenth anniversary of the foundation of the Gestoras was celebrated with much splendour. The comprehensive programme, stretching over several days and covering the entire area of the Basque region, included a sizeable international congress on torture and repression, self-confinements, human chains, poster campaigns, exhibitions, film performances, commemorations for killed and missing Etarras, telegram campaigns for prisoners and visits to prisons, festivities and festivals.[17] According to the organizers the success of the amnesty days was considerable. No less than 12,000 people are said to have participated in the self-confinement campaign in fifty places, which proves the mobilization capability of this branch of the nationalist movement as well as the continuous, enormously emotional support in the region for detainees and fugitives.

Political pressure and resistance

The above arguments might convey the impression that the Basque region was occupied by radical-nationalist groups, and that the overwhelming majority of the population were overtly or secretly associated with ETA. This would be an incorrect conclusion as can be seen by reference to the broad political spectrum of opinions in the region as reflected in the poll reported on p. 7–8, as well as to the fact that HB is backed by only a little over 15 per cent of the voters. The militant left nationalists form a minority – a very aggressive one to be sure – which aims to expand its influence at the expense of other political parties and groups.

This expansive pressure is felt in various ways. The murder attempts of ETA are the most spectacular and at the same time the most disgraceful form. Only in the past were attempts exclusively directed against the exponents of the central state, such as police officers and military governors. Nowadays no Basque, irrespective of walk of life, family, or praiseworthy actions for the benefit of the people, is immune against punitive actions of the terror organization. Even former Etarras who have withdrawn from the organization are in danger of revenge. HB as an ETA-oriented party thus has at its disposal a very effective weapon with which to silence political opponents if they are unable to win them over to their way of thinking.

Basque employers, company executives and wealthy, independent professional men are to an especially high degree exposed to the intimidations and threats of ETA. ETA demands that they contribute to the preservation of the organization and the financing of its activities by paying a 'revolution tax' (*impuesto revolucionario*). It is difficult to give concrete data about the compulsory money levied in this way.[18] Lists of 'tax payers' found by the police in French hiding places of the terrorists indicate that the tribute system has until recently worked well and has enabled the violent organizations to accumulate a yearly income running into millions. Apart from the direct financial blood-letting suffered by the Basque economy, the socio-psychological consequences of a social climate of fear and extortion in which wealthy Basques live should not be underestimated. Around 5,000 of them are said to have turned their backs on their homeland[19], with the result that for the first time a certain lack of initiative is discernible in the private business sphere in an area traditionally rich in enterprising talents.

The recourse to violence as a means for the enforcement of ideological and partly pragmatic aims is, however, limited not only to ETA but also characterizes, though less strikingly, the legal wing of the radical-nationalist movement. The socialists, the only all-Spanish party continuously controlling a considerable regular voting population, are those who have to bear the brunt of their intolerance and resentments. Anonymous threatening letters to PSOE politicians and nightly phone calls at their homes are no rarity. Town councillors of the party have been subjected to insults and indignities and their cars and homes demolished; sometimes they have had to suffer physical assault. The headquarters of the party (*casa del pueblo*) were besmeared with ETA emblems and frequently exposed to attacks. Only recently Basque teenagers threw Molotov cocktails into the bar of a *casa del pueblo*, injuring a number of persons, some of them seriously.[20]

Although discernible in all the three Basque provinces, the impact of the political pressure is especially plain in the province of Guipuzcoa, where the majority of ETA members originate. There, many policemen have been killed in the so-called death triangle (between the towns of Zarauz, Tolosa and Fuenterabia). In some towns (such as Rentéria and Hernani) the terror organization enjoys such a strong backing that it, or rather its political representative (HB), was temporarily in a position, as may be the case in a 'freed zone', politically and deliberately to do as they liked. As this is also the province which in the 1960s and 1970s absorbed a disproportionate number of Spanish immigrants, tension and conflict over Basque interests are pre-programmed, in spite of the relatively open-minded attitude of the immigrants. The language and flag issues as well as the distribution of representation in the town councils are some of the causes for conflicts on the local scene. It is not just that the Basque language, the Euskadi, should enjoy the same rights as Castilian, or that the Basque flag be hoisted beside the Spanish flag; HB and its followers demand that the Basque language *only* should be used in schools and that the Basque flag *only* be hoisted: conditions which the representatives of the immigrants are unable and refuse to accept. As these issues are decided in the town council, appointments to this body are of utmost importance. HB sympathizers react particularly vehemently if their group is in danger of losing the majority in the town council and the election of a socialist, possibly even non-Basque, mayor is under discussion. There have been instances in which angry followers of the party coalition minority have entered the town hall forcibly, interrupted the election procedure and tried to deter the unwanted candidate from assuming the office, threatening him with the call, 'ETA, kill him!'.[21]

Furthermore, considering that the left-nationalist movement has at its disposal a potential political mobilization far in excess of that of the other parties and that it is permanently present in the public life of Euskadis, particularly in its squares and streets by means of demonstrations, rallies, marches and other protest actions, it becomes obvious why its political influence so far exceeds its limited numerical size. It profits from the fact that the Basques have preserved certain traits of a traditional community: a high degree of social control, deriving from a failure to separate and distinguish the private and intimate from the public and collective spheres on the one hand,[22] and a great informal communication compactness of the Basque society on the other. Though the vigorous control of the individual by the community may enhance the power of resistance and survival of the ethnic entity, under conditions of external threat it will become a burden if the population is split in its political attitude, as is the case at present. It does produce pressure of conformity; it compels the individual to put his cards on the table, bearing in mind that his reactions and statements will rapidly be passed on. HB and its radical followers make use of this for their purposes: they aim at an informal control monopoly over Basque society and naturally they are more successful in villages and smaller towns than in cities like Bilbao and San Sebastian.

The reaction of the other Basques to the vociferous and militant hegemonic claims of the radical-nationalist bloc shows itself in rejection and insecurity, sometimes in sympathy and last but not least in fear. Though fear, first of all, stems from the risk that an incautious remark or an action displeasing the HB followers might provoke an attack, e.g. endanger life and limb, it is not exhausted in this physical dimension. There is also, social fear, as well as the fear that if one holds a divergent political opinion one may be depicted by the left nationalists as an enemy or traitor to the Basque cause, or be socially marginalized by friends and acquaintances.[23] In order to evade social ostracism, many Basques keep silent over ETA manœuvres and the intolerant political plots of HB and adjust themselves externally, though internally they do not at all sanction them. This compulsory solidarity, imposed not only by the radical minority on the majority but by many Basques themselves, explains rather odd actions, as in the behaviour of a wealthy Basque kidnapped by ETA who, after his release upon payment of a very high ransom, had nothing but praise for his extortioners and under no circumstances wanted them to be put on trial.

But not all keep silent and accept without contradiction the raids of a minority grimly intent on the justness of its cause. There have always been individuals who refused to give in to ETA threats and to pay the demanded amount. Fatal assaults on innocent citizens, the political sense of which no one understood, have been followed by repeated public declarations of disgust and appeals to ETA to stop its insane murderous activities. For a long time these protests were marginal occurrences in the region and it is only very recently that a compact front to resist the continuation of terror acts seems to have taken shape. After the raid on the local PSOE (Socialist Party of Spain) headquarters, in the course of which a number of people were seriously injured, there were vigorous and massive protest demonstrations. Following the murder of a policeman married to a Basque woman, a general strike took place in a village in Guipuzcoa[24], for the first time indicating disapproval of this act instead of solidarity with it. Even the high clergy, a very influential moral authority in this profoundly Catholic region, is becoming increasingly critical towards the track of blood left by ETA. The unanimous condemnation of three particularly brutal attacks voiced by all parties (except HB) and the majority of the political representatives leaves no doubt of the beginnings of a change in mood of the public. This change of mood does not reflect a sudden about-face of the Basques or their political representatives, but appears primarily to be connected with the weakened position of ETA. This is mainly due to the strategy pursued by the Spanish government in the fight against terrorism to which we will now turn in conclusion.

MEASURES TAKEN BY THE SPANISH GOVERNMENT AGAINST ETA

The policy of restraining political violence in the Basque region, employed by the PSOE government in Madrid since the early 1980s, is a combination of control measures aimed at overcoming and depriving ETA of its power, and the beginnings of reconciliation with the Basque people, including its radical groups. The Spanish government has improved its prosecution apparatus and is, above all, anxious to achieve collaboration with the French security authorities in order to drive ETA into a tactical defensive. These efforts were successful for the first time, as a result of which ETA was compelled to give up its base in the Basque region of southern France. The halting dialogue between the Spanish Ministry of the Interior and ETA which began in 1984 as well as the very recent attempt at a general reconciliation between the government in Madrid and the political forces in the Basque region are foremost among the 'positive' initiatives.

If the significance of the southern French area for the terror organization is appreciated, then it will become evident how great an importance the Spanish government attached to convincing Paris of the necessity of joint action against Basque terrorism.[25] As early as the 1960s the first Etarras evaded the repressive reach of the Franco regime by withdrawing into that region, which presented itself as an ideal vanishing area thanks to its proximity to Spain and the close ethnic connection with its population. But its role as a retreat zone for Basque rebels in distress did not end here; the area around Biarritz, Bayonne, and St. Jean-de-Luz developed into a regeneration area for the Basque activists and ultimately became the central starting position for most of their raids. After the ETA leadership had established its headquarters there, it created an infrastructure of its own, consisting of ideological and military training centres, arms depots, a car park, offices, archives, and the like. This could happen with the knowledge of the French authorities; used to the practice of generously granting asylum during the Franco dictatorship they did not see any reason to take steps against fugitive ETA members residing in French territory. But even after Franco's death and the transition to a new parliamentary system of government in Spain, and for a long time, France refrained from taking steps to deprive the Etarras of the right of sanctuary. The French government received sceptically the argument brought forward by the Spanish government that yesterday's freedom fighters should today be rated as dangerous terrorists murdering innocent people, because it had certain doubts as to the profoundness of the democratic change in the southern neighbouring country – doubts which were also nourished by rumours about cases of torture in Spanish prisons. It was not until 1984 that the socialist prime minister, Felipe Gonzales, succeeded in the course of negotiations with his French counterpart François Mitterand to achieve an initial breakthrough in respect to the problems of the Basque terrorists. France started, hesitantly, to extradite Etarras or to deport them to third countries, a practice more vigorously continued by Jacques Chirac and culminating, in 1987, in raid-like detention campaigns, which brought about the mopping-up of the area of Etarras and their families. The reasons for this about-face in Paris with regard to the handling of sanctuary permits are manifold: partly connected with the fact that Spain has proved to be a democratic country and the taint of the authoritarian political past has definitely been eradicated (at least since its incorporation within the framework of the European Community); partly due to the rise of terrorism in France's own Basque region by way of 'Action Directe' which, for the first time, confronts France with the problem of terrorism; and also to the diplomatic pressure exerted by countries such as the Federal Republic of Germany and the USA with a view to bringing about collaboration in the struggle against terrorism. The revocation of the right of sanctuary of the Etarras in southern France had catastrophic consequences for the terror organization. In one day, so to speak, it lost its main foothold and co-ordination centre; its infrastructure was destroyed and its leaders dispersed over several continents. In short it was extremely weakened.

This set-back struck at a time when ETA was increasingly running into trouble inside Spain. The Spanish government has spared no effort to improve upon the laws against terrorism and to increase the efficiency of the security authorities entrusted with persecuting them. During 1984 the existing regulations against terrorism were intensified: the sentences against political violators were increased, a number of offences pertaining to terrorism were decreed (such as the propagation and justification of terrorist actions), and the period of detention of persons suspected by the police of terrorism was prolonged to ten days. During this time the accused was removed from any external contact and had no possibility of soliciting a judge to verify the legitimacy of his arrest, and therefore critics reproached the government for opening the door to the abuse of police power in a variety of ways, including torture. In order to obtain the speedy and fair trial of accused Etarras, a special court has been established for them far away from the Basque region where most of the incriminating terror acts are perpetrated. Madrid's distrust of the Basque judiciary, manifested in this settlement, has for a long time also guided its attitude towards the Basque police, as provided for in the autonomy legislation of 1979. The organization and development of the Basque police authorities was delayed out of fear that their attitude towards ETA might be too lenient, that the violent organization might infiltrate their ranks and, worst of all, might serve as a national Basque liberation force rebelling against the supremacy of Madrid. For all these reasons the central government preferred to leave the responsibility for the fight against terrorism in the hands of the all-Spanish police force, including the Civil Guard (Guardia civil), which has been singularly detested in the Basque region since the Franco era. However, the Spanish judiciary, by persistently investigating complaints made by detained Basques against police infringements, regardless of and despite the rancour of the Minister of the Interior, effectively counterbalances the central mechanism built up by the Madrid government, whose declared policy is the elimination of terrorism and whose pressure is also felt by numerous innocent Basques. As a matter of fact, the Constitutional Court, in a recent judgement, censured several unconstitutional regulations of the anti-terrorism law and demanded their revision. Meanwhile, however, the Spanish government has, of its own will, announced the abrogation of the special law or rather its integration in the general criminal law, and has switched over to a more liberal handling of the Basque problem, resorting to a lesser degree to the persecution machinery of the police. This ties in with the accent on the second component of the policy of the central government *vis-à-vis* the small region, which is to focus on dialogue and increased collaboration with the Basque political forces.

This preparedness for dialogue also includes ETA. The first contacts between government representatives and the terror organization occurred in the mid-1980s. The talks between them were interrupted several times but always renewed. The government has based its policy on the assumption that, in view of the weakened position of ETA and the increasingly desperate plight of these few members who are still free and whose lives, moreover, are threatened by assaults of a right-extremist organization (GAL), the ETA leadership would have no alternative but to enter into a dialogue with Madrid in order to negotiate an honourable withdrawal and to achieve immunity from sanctions for those who want to return to civil life. This assumption sounds so plausible that the public always attaches great hopes to the renewal of the talks between the two parties. But two considerations have repeatedly impeded the continuation of the talks and appear to jeopardize their success in future. First, the terror organization is in the habit of perpetrating particularly spectacular and brutal assaults during these dialogues. This may point to the existence of a hard wing inside ETA, aiming at torpedoing a peace agreement by all means, but, more probably, should be interpreted as a demonstration of the organization's strength in order to obtain greater concessions from Madrid. In fact, these assaults make it difficult for the government to justify the continuation of the dialogue with 'murderers' *vis-à-vis* the public opinion of the country. The second reason refers to the nature of the dialogue, which the government presents as mere talks, but which ETA interprets as 'negotiations'. The different terms used are not significant linguistically, but rather highlight the different political viewpoints. As a matter of fact, the term 'negotiations' underlines the political character of these talks, which is also reflected by the fact that ETA is reluctant to accept less than at least a partial realization of its political demands included in the 'Alternative KAS'. The government, on the other hand, puts the accent on the smoothest possible return of the Etarras into the civil society, thus playing down the political content of the contacts.

Since the talks with the terror organization are not proceeding satisfactorily, the Spanish government is making efforts to establish a parallel contact with the Basque parties, hoping to isolate ETA politically and to drive it into social solitude. This is not a new approach, however. In the early 1980s Felipe Gonzales, the Spanish Prime Minister, proposed to the civil parties in the Basque region that they reach an understanding with the Spanish government on the basis of a minimal accord on values, but in vain. At that time there still prevailed a feeling of solidarity for ETA and therefore protests were voiced with regard to the forthcoming (already apparent) extradition agreement between Spain and France. But meanwhile a change of mind among the civil political forces in the Basque region has been taking place, caused by the obvious weakening of ETA and the increasing brutality and arbitrariness of its violence, as well as the breaking up of PNV, which makes the support of the government by what is left of PNV possible only at the cost of a coalition with Felipe Gonzales' party, the socialists. Gonzales, for one, is making concessions to the public opinion in the Basque region, now promising the rapid enlargement of the Basque police forces and, as already hinted, announcing the integration of the anti-terrorist law into the common criminal law. It is this political background which enables us to understand the declaration (in December 1987) published by fourteen Spanish and Basque parties, which were joined by a multitude of political groups in the Basque region.

Is this proof that the anti-terrorist initiatives and measures of the Spanish government are successful? Is there a foreseeable end to the blood-shedding by ETA and the subsequent repressive counter-blows of the police? While the first question may be answered with a cautious 'yes', there still are doubts with regard to the possibility of a definite end to terrorist violence. These doubts are partly linked with the double strategy of the government (an increased operative encirclement and restraining of the terror organization together with the beginning of a dialogue with it) and partly with the existence of a widely ramified network of groups of sympathizers, as outlined on pp. 9–24. The intensification of the pressure of harassment by the Spanish police, combined with the revocation by France of the traditional ETA refuge has in fact, led to the smashing of most of the cadres and operation cells of the organization and has thus considerably reduced its disposing capacity. Despite this, the number of attacks and above all victims has not perceptibly lessened (see Figure 1.1). As a rule, recourse to violence, is a sign of a lack of resources and real or imaginary distress, as indicated by the case of the Basque region under Franco. Through the accentuation of this situation, namely increasingly cornering the terrorists, terrorism may temporarily be reduced but not definitely checked. Rather, in the absence of thorough preparation and control of the activities, enhanced brutality of the attacks for example a larger number of unintended victims, should be taken into account. As to the dialogue between the Spanish government and ETA, it should be borne in mind that apart from all other objections raised to it – including the argument that it goes beyond the mandate of a democratically elected government and might influence other groups too to resort to illegal methods of pressure[26] – it amounts to corroboration of the usurped role of political spokesman which ETA claims for itself in respect of the Basque region. Why, after all, should the terror organization voluntarily relinquish future terrorist attacks, when this same dialogue confirms its always repeated thesis, that only force of arms will bring the political adversary to the negotiating table? The strategy of enhanced control as well as of dialogue with the terror organization, as analysed on pp. 9–24, does not take into consideration the fact that ETA is supported by a large radical nationalist movement in the Basque region. Even if the ETA leadership were coming round, it would by no means signify that all the groups of its followers accepted the new appeasement trend. The third initiative of the Spanish government, a gradual rapprochement and reconciliation with the moderate forces in the Basque region, appears to be the most promising one to achieve the gradual political and social isolation of ETA. It is particularly important to equip the Basque executive with the competence and instruments necessary to mould the co-ordinating body into an authority which is capable of making binding decisions and of implementing them: with its own criminal investigation department and security police, its own prosecutors and law-courts – in short with an independent sanctions machinery[27]. Only when the Basque executive is empowered to rid itself of the unfortunate role of buffer between Madrid and the national radical camp, only then it will be able to mobilize the support and loyalty of the Basque people necessary to put an effective check to the hegemonic claim of the 'counter-state' ETA and its radical followers.[28]

ACKNOWLEDGEMENTS

I would like to extend my sincere thanks to Ludger Mees and Roland Ostermann for their assistance in compiling and preparing the material. Most of the following statements are based on the analysis of Spanish and Basque daily and weekly newspapers, especially *El País*, *Cambio 16*, *EGIN* and *Punto y Hora* (the latter two are identified with the radical nationalist movement). The exact references are stated in cases of specially pointed statements or important dates or empiric circumstances.

NOTES

1   Compare, Corcuera, Javier, *Orígenes, Ideología y Organización del Nacional-ismo Vasco (1876–1904)*, Madrid, 1979; Elorza, Antonio, *Ideologias del Nacionalismo Vasco 1876–1937*, San Sebastian, 1978; Larronde, Jean

Claude, *El Nacionalismo Vasco. Su origen y su ideología en la obra de Sabino Araña-Goiri*, San Sebastian, 1977; Solozabal, Juan José, *el Premier Nacionalismo Vasco*, Madrid, 1975; Payne, Stanley, *El Nacionalismo Vasco. De sus origenes a la ETA*, Barcelona, 1974.

2 See, Nuñez, Luis C., *La Sociedad Vasca Actual*, San Sebastian, 1977; Nuñez, Luis C., *Clases Sociales en Euskadi*, San Sebastian, 1977; Azaola, José Miguel de, *Vasconia y su Destino*, 2 Vols, Madrid, 1976; Clark, Robert P., *The Basques: The Franco Years and Beyond*, Reno, Nevada, 1979; Lang, Josef, *Das baskische Labyrinth. Unterdrückung und Widerstand in Euskadi*, Frankfurt, 1983; Waldmann, Peter, 'Sozio-ökonomischer Wandel, zentralistische Unterdrückung und Protestegewalt im Baskenland', in Waldmann *et al.*, *Die geheime Dynamik autoritærer Diktaturen*, Schriften der Philosophischen Fakultæten der Universitæt Augsburg, No. 22, München, 1982, pp. 199–285.

3 Waldmann, Peter, 'Katalonien und Baskenland: Historische Entwicklung der nationalistischen Bewegungen und Formen des Widerstands in der Franco-Zeit', in Waldmann *et al.* (eds.), *Sozialer Wandel und Herrschaft im Spanien Francos*, Paderborn, 1984, pp. 155 ff., 184 ff.

4 In my opinion, *The Basque Insurgents: ETA 1952–1980*, by Robert P. Clark, is the best book written about ETA. Also see Jauregui Bereciartu, Gurutz, *Ideología y Estrategia Política de ETA. Analisis de su Evolucíon entre 1959 y 1968*, Madrid, 1981; Garmendia, José Mari, *Historia de ETA*, 2 vols, San Sebastian 1979/1980; Aranzadi, Juan, *Milenarismo Vasco. Edad do oro, etnia y nativismo*, Madrid 1987, as well as the references enumerated in note 2.

5 This is Alfonso Perez-Agote's thesis, 'La Reproduccíon del Nacionalismo: El Caso Vasco, Madrid, 1984, p. 85 ff.

6 About the Basque party system compare: Cibrían, Ramiro, 'El sistema electoral y de Partidos en Euzkadi, Papers. *Revista do Sociologia*, 14 (1980), p. 87; Llera Ramo, Francisco José, 'El Sistema do Partidos Vasco: Distancia Ideologíca y Legitimacíon Política', *Revista Española de Investigaciones Sociologicas*, 28 (October–December 1984), pp. 171–206; Corcuera Atienza, Javier *et al.*, 'Sistema do Partidos, Instituciones y Comunidad Nacionalista en Euskadi', *Revista de Politica Comparada*, October 1980, pp. 155–90; Buse, Michael, *Die Neue Spanische Demokratie. Parteiensystem und Wæhlerorintierungen 1976–1984*, Baden-Baden 1985, p. 227 ff.

7 Compare the definition in Lang op. cit., p. 325 and *Cambio 16*, 731, 2 December 1985, p. 42, though they differ slightly from each other.

8 Compare *El País* 14 March 1987, pp. 1, 14 ff. *Cambio 16*, 731, 1 June 1987, p. 28 ff.; *Cambio 16*, 830, 26 October 1987, p. 26 ff.; and *El País*, 27 December 1987, p. 15.

9 See abstracts and comments in *El País*, 1 December and 2 December 1987 as well as *Süddeutsche Zeitung*, 2 December 1984, pp. 2, 4.

10 Waldmann, Peter, 'Mitgliederstruktur, Sozalisationsmedien u. gesellschaftlicher Rückhalt der baskischen ETA, *Politische Vierteljahresschrift*, Vol. 22, 1, April 1981, pp. 45 ff., 63; Porta, Donatella and Mattina, Liborio, 'Ciclos Politícos y Movilizacíon Etnica: El Caso Vasco', *Revista*

Espanola de Investigaciones Sociologicas, 35 (1986), pp. 123–48 especially pp. 141 ff.

11   Laraña Rodriguez-Cabello, Enrique, 'Desencanto, Crisis de Autoridad y Nacionalismo en la Evolucíon Politíca del País Vasco', *Revista Internacional de Sociologia*, Vol. 40 (1982), p. 101 ff.

12   Compare *El País* 13 September 1987, p. 14 and J. Lang, op. cit., pp. 356 ff.

13   In addition see Blasco, Rogelio, 'Nueve Rock Vasco: Un Fenómeno Sociológico. Cuadernos de Alzate', *Revista Vasca de la Cultura y las Ideas*, 6 (April–September 1987), pp. 12–29; also compare the informative, journalistic report about the radicalism of the Basque youth in *El País*, 1 December 1986, p. 19.

14   J. Lang, op. cit., p. 73.

15   The following exposition is based on the analysis of relevant reports in *Egin* and the weekly *Punto y Hora*.

16   The largest and best known is the journey to the high security prison Herrera in the Mancha, taking place annually on 26 December, where more than half of the detained Etarras are imprisoned. In 1986, 7,000 Basques travelled by bus to this prison, which is nearly 700 km from the Basque region. The figure for 1987 is estimated to be the same. See, *Punto y Hora*, 499, 17–24 December 1987, pp. 22 ff.

17   A considerable number of Basques travelled as far as Paris and hung a banner on the Eiffel Tower demanding amnesty for Basque detainees. It was the purpose of this action to draw the attention of international and particularly French public opinion to the continued oppression of the Spanish Basque. See, *Punto y Hora*, 499, pp. 6 ff.

18   The evaluation of the presumed income of the violent organization (from kidnappings, bank robberies and revolution tax) can be found in an article published in *Cambio 16*, 801, 6 April 1987. Also compare *El País*, 26 March 1986, p. 53.

19   According to the information given by the Secretary of the Chamber of Industry and Commerce in Bilbao, in the spring of 1986. Also see the report on the economic situation in the Basque region, based on competent documentary evidence, published in *Ya*, 6 January 1987, p. 26.

20   Compare reports on 'The Attempt of Portugalete' in *El País*, 28 April 1987. One of the consequences not so much noticed of the militancy of the left-nationalists and Basque ethnocentrism is the fact that Spanish policemen employed in the region and exposed to rejection and ostracism frequently commit suicide. See the relevant item in *El País*, 19 July 1987.

21   *Cambio 16*, 607, 18 July 1983, pp. 25 ff.

22   A. Pérez-Agote, op. cit., pp. 126 ff.

23   The Society for Human Rights in the Basque region organized a competition among pupils in secondary schools for stories about human rights. The prize-winning story dealt with a murder attempt by an ETA group, of which the narrator became an involuntary witness. It is significant that in the following conscientious conflict about whether he should prevent the murder, it is not the fear for his own life which is

dominant but rather the fear that in the future he might be considered a traitor (*chivato*). See *Cambio 16*, 796, 2 March 1987, p. 28.

24   It concerns the little town of Ordizia in Guipuzcoa. A woman of this village, formerly a leading member of ETA (Yoyes), from which she resigned in order to take up studies but who never voiced any critical remarks in respect of the terror organization, was murdered by an ETA commando in the autumn of 1986 on her way to a festival in her home town as an act of revenge and for the purpose of deterrence. The case *per se* and the aggravating accompanying circumstances of the crime (the woman, carrying a child in her arms, was participating in a procession) stirred excitement and led to the formation of a resistance group against the murderous actions of the ETA. After the attempt against the Spanish policeman, whose wife belongs to a well known nationalist family, this group has expanded into a regular local resistance front. See the article in *El Diario Vasco*, 15 November 1987, p. 4.

25   R. P. Clark, op. cit., 1984, pp. 205–15.

26   In addition to this see the article of Ramon Garcia Cotarelo in *Cambio 16*, 771, 8 September 1986, and of Ramon Jauregui Atondo in *El País*, 17 September 1986.

27   Relevant also to the proposal of the international expert commission convened by the Spanish government in 1985, to give its opinion concerning violence in the Basque region. Ministerio del Interior y Justicía del Gabierno Vasco, *Informe de la Comisíon Internacional sobre la Violencia eu El País Vasco*, Vitoria 1986, especially Chapter 9.

28   The thesis of Alejandro Muñoz Alonso, 'El Terrorismo en España', Madrid, 1982, pp. 217 ff., that ETA is a counter state *in nuce* appears to be correct.

Chapter 2

The terrorist lobby in West Germany: campaigns and propaganda in support of terrorism

Hans Joseph Horchem

For over fifteen years the Federal Republic of Germany has lived with terrorist attacks. It cannot be foreseen when this particular kind of criminality will end. Most attacks come from the Rote Armee Fraktion (RAF) and the Revolutionaere Zellen (Revolutionary Cells or RZ). The third German terrorist group, the 2nd June Movement, was dissolved in spring 1980. The members of the Berlin element of this organization joined the RZ. The greater part of membership was taken over by the RAF. In the course of the years both the composition of the sympathizers and supporters of German terrorism and the way in which they provide their support have changed.

When the RAF, with its concept of the 'armed struggle', became public knowledge, it attracted first the attention, and later the sympathy, of a large number of intellectuals. This lasted mainly until the RAF moved on from simple logistic operations (the procurement of money, vehicles, weapons and personal documentation) to attacks in the course of which individuals were killed and wounded. Afterwards, admittedly, they continued to enjoy understanding for their objectives on the part of their original sympathizers, but not for their acts of violence. Sympathizers who until then had given voice to the same aims as those of the RAF masked their continued intellectual support by criticizing alleged attacks on the part of the security authorities. In this way they made a contribution to the excusing of violence on the part of the RAF. As they saw it, the RAF were only using 'counter-violence' against unjustified violence on the part of the state.

After 1977 this sort of transferred sympathy could not longer be justified. In that year the Federal Attorney General, Siegfried

Buback, the banker Jürgen Ponto and the Employers' President Hanns Martin Schleyer were murdered. The RAF found support for their activities only from individuals who could be considered to belong to the 'New Left'.

Even this group of sympathizers dwindled after the RAF, on 7 August 1985, shot and killed the American soldier Edward Pimental in order to obtain his identity card. On 8 August, with the help of this document, they obtained entry to the American air base at the Rhein/Main airfield in Frankfurt and there carried out a serious bomb attack. The murder of the American soldier led to severe criticism of the New Left. This criticism has continued until this day and reached a peak in the course of heated discussions at the so-called 'Frankfurt Congress' on 1–2 February 1986. Since then, the RAF has mainly enjoyed support only from individuals who consider themselves as belonging to the 'legal arm' of the organisation.

The RZ, which have developed since 1971, tried right from the beginning to set themselves apart from the RAF. Contrary to RAF theory, according to which the student elite determines the revolution, the RZ wanted a return to the masses. This would come about by associating individual revolutionary acts with concrete social-political conflicts.[1] Basically, RZ attacks were not directed against human beings, but against inanimate targets. Because of this distinction RZ attacks for a long time found more sympathy with the public than did the brutal RAF attacks. In 1984, however, the RZ were criticised in New Left magazines. The commentators in question wondered what twelve years, during which the RZ had carried out acts of violence, had achieved for the revolutionary situation. For a period of almost two years, they were preoccupied by the discussion of the question whether in the long run subversive operations might not have better prospects of success rather than attacks with explosives. During this discussions phase, the RZ carried out virtually no attacks.[2]

By far the greater proportion of support activity and propaganda actions for German terrorism was intended on behalf of the RAF rather than the RZ. For that reason the following consideration is directed principally towards this branch of the terrorist lobby.

THE BEGINNINGS

From the very beginning, the left and liberal intelligentsia went along with the protest movement in the Federal Republic of Germany that started in the mid-1960s. The model for the German student protest was the protest movement in the USA, which concentrated on opposition to American involvement in Vietnam. Television broadcasts of mass demonstrations by students in the USA, which reached their peak at Berkeley 1964, gave impetus to student movements in France, Italy and Germany. Even before this, there had existed close scientific contacts between the east-coast universities and the university high schools in California and German universities, particularly with Berlin. Arising from the protest movements in the USA and Europe, the New Left movement came to wide public notice with a time delay of about two years. Core groups formulated the protest. Students tested and further developed the forms of protest.

Those elements within the universities concerned with politics, sociology and psychology, i.e. those faculties in which criticism of society was taught formed the reservoir for the demonstration. Many students were influenced by the theories of Herbert Marcuse. Hundreds of young people attended the lectures given by Professors Adorno and Horckheimer in Frankfurt.

The Great Coalition between the CDU and the SPD in 1965 gave a new thrust to the protest movement. Young people in the Federal Republic saw this alliance as a betrayal of democracy. For them, it was a confirmation of their suspicion that the new German state was basically rotten and sclerotic, and that the 'rulers' were trying to maintain their power by authoritarian means.

The student youth movement, with the support of a vociferous segment of liberal and left-wing professors, joined in the campaign against the emergency laws. The 1968 Easter attacks, which were directed mainly against the Springer Publishing House, coincided with this phase. At the same time, a debate on violence was developing. One justification theory differentiated between violence against things and violence against people. Violence against things was justified as a weapon in the struggle by minorities against repression and against state institutions that exercise repression. Even at this time, however, the dialectical quality of such theories of justification was apparent. It did not exclude violence against persons in the future.

In August 1968 the Warsaw Pact troops invaded Czechoslovakia. In autumn 1968 the campaign against the emergency laws collapsed. The students' protest movement split up into basic groups who turned to instruction in Marxist theory and to discussion of the social analysis of the Federal Republic and the revolutionary organization they were striving to build. Three years later, in February 1971, the RAF emerged out from this transitional phase, armed with the concept of the armed struggle.

Many liberal and left-wing intellectuals declared this concept to be a necessary consequence of the failed protest movement, which they said had been forcibly suppressed by the establishment. They failed to recognize that, both in theory and strategy, the RAF had already taken the next step from demonstration to acts of violence.

The first operations of the RAF were aimed at creating a logistical basis for future operations. The great majority of finance was obtained by means of armed bank robbery. During the build-up phase, on 29 September 1970, there were three bank raids in Berlin, carried out at the same time of the day. In all 220,000 DM fell into the perpetrators' hands.

Sympathizers welcomed these operations. Even among the general public, those who were not politically committed hesitated to condemn them as criminal acts. The obviously meticulous preparation and the precision and daring of the execution of the raids attracted admiration. The terrorists were looked upon as a new type of Robin Hood bandits. In this scenario, the police officers played the role of the corrupt Sheriff of Nottingham. From this mentality, there developed support actions by individuals who did not belong to the RAF and most of whom today find it impossible to understand their former involvement.

In November 1970, Professor Peter Brückner put a flat in Hanover at the disposal of Ulrike Meinhof and two other members of the RAF. From 24 December 1970 until 8 January 1971 a teacher at a secondary school in Stuttgart let other members of the RAF use his flat. In January 1971, another teacher in Stuttgart accepted packages from RAF members and later delivered them to other members of the RAF. In February 1971, a doctor from Heidelberg rented a safe flat in Hamburg for the RAF. In mid-March 1971, another teacher from Stuttgart put his car at the disposal of the RAF. At the end of March 1971, a doctor in Hamburg rented a flat for Gudrun Ensslin. In September 1971, an actor from the Stuttgart State Theatre rented a car and put it at the disposal of the RAF. In January 1972, a psychologist from Esslingen rented a safe flat for the RAF in Frankfurt. The apartment was used until June 1972.

These acts of support by uncommitted citizens are only examples of the many other instances of assistance lent to the terrorists during the early phase of their operations. Their support was made easier in many cases by a fixed ideological commitment to political programmes and the subjective impression that they were living in a state that was not free of repression. The RAF activists used this type of solidarity for the most part without giving it a second thought, often concealing as well their own identity and their true intentions. In many cases the sympathizers showed uncertainty about their own viewpoint and an inadequate grasp of reality. They unhesitatingly gave support for criminal activities, the quality of which they could not understand because of their own ideologically inflexible convictions.

This type of sympathizer greatly hampered investigations by the security authorities. The climate of publicity that resulted from such sympathies highlighted the problems fully. In many newspaper articles the behaviour of the sympathizers was explained by comparison to the Gestapo era, during which citizens gave refuge to resistance fighters fleeing from the police pursuing them. Differences in attitudes in the media were reflected according to whether the RAF were called the 'Baader-Meinhof Gang' or the 'Baader-Meinhof Group.'

The German Nobel Prize-winner Heinrich Böll wrote an essay in *Der Spiegel* on 10 January 1972 about the RAF and Ulrike Meinhof under the title 'Suddenly, so much love. Does Ulrike Meinhof want a pardon or safe conduct?!'. The article reached its peak with the controversial proposition that 60 million people (the population of the Federal Republic) were hunting a handful of young people.[3]

THE FIRST MURDERS

In 1972 the RAF moved away from the logistics and the publicizing of the aims of their struggle to offensive action, although many of their members had already been arrested.

The series of bomb-attacks – fifteen explosive devices in six locations – began on 11 May 1972 with an attack on the Headquarters of the 5th US Corps in Frankfurt. One American officer was killed. On 15 May 1972, attacks on the Land Criminal Office in Munich and on the Police Headquarters in Augsburg followed. On 19 May 1972, 38 people were injured, some of whom seriously, from the detonation of two bombs in the Springer Publishing House in Hamburg. On 24 May 1972, a heavy attack on the Headquarters of the American

Army in Europe in Heidelberg took place, resulting in the death of three soldiers.

These attacks were clearly no random terrorism, but deliberately calculated actions, the nature of which was intended to cause other organizations and groups of the New Left to align themselves with the RAF. Therefore, the RAF squad that was responsible for the attack on the Springer Publishing House emphasized that a warning had been given to the publishing firm so that the building could be evacuated. The attack against the police and against American institutions, of which no advance warning was given, not only foresaw that human beings would be killed, but actually included that fact in their calculations. They aimed thereby at achieving solidarity among other factions of the revolutionary movement.

Such solidarity did not occur, which was, to a certain extent, also a result of errors in the theoretical self-portrayal of the RAF. These shortcomings, which were already apparent at that time, have continued and further developed to this day. Later, the RAF compensated for the increasing weakness in their attempts at self-justification by means of increased brutality.

From the very beginning, the RAF faced the dilemma that, while wanting to struggle for the working class, they had hardly any members who could be considered belonging to the working class. For it was clear to the members of the RAF that the leadership of a revolution, such as that for which they were working, must, according to Lenin, belong to the enlightened part of the worker's class. To this very day, this thesis has never been openly discussed by the members of the RAF. Only Horst Mahler, at a very early stage, drew a theoretical conclusion, namely, explaining that the industrial proletariat in capitalist countries had evolved into a 'worker's aristocracy'. Thus, the proletariat could not be a 'revolutionary subject' for the RAF. On that basis, Mahler focused on those parts of the intelligentsia that were concerned and worried by the fact 'that the stratum of society from which they came had to a much larger extent than previously been threatened, or even overtaken, by the process of declassification'. To this revolutionary intelligentsia Mahler allocated the function of an *avant-garde*. It was not the industrial labourer, but the revolutionary elements in the student body, who were the present-day custodians of contemporary conscience.[4]

The task of the student elite – to work for the interests of labour (and not capital) – had, in the eyes of many intellectuals, been betrayed by the attack on the Springer Publishing House. While Springer itself was accepted as a target for revolutionary attacks, the workers who worked in the publishing and printing jobs were not.

Renato Curcio, the leading thinker of the Italian terrorist organization Red Brigades, recognized the difficulties within the German group arising from this context. In a letter from prison in December 1974, he stated that the RAF had made the mistake of starting the argument too early and on too many levels. In addition, the RAF had not recognized the 'real interests of the Movement'.[5] In a further letter from prison, in March 1975, Curcio voiced the criticism that the RAF had begun the build-up of their organization outside the Movement, and that the 'question of the workers' had apparently not been acknowledged by the RAF.[6] This reproach – that the RAF was lacking communication with the 'masses' – was one of the main obstacles against a closer co-operation between Red Brigades and the RAF in the following years.

In 1979 Horst Mahler, in a discussion with Stephan Aust, said that the bomb attack on the Springer Publishing House in Hamburg had represented a turning-point in the development of the RAF:

The most obvious thing was the attack on the Springer building in Hamburg, where workers and office staff were injured, and where, by the size of the attack, much worse could have happened. It was abundantly clear that this way of going about things was something quite separate from what we had jointly envisaged under *modus operandi*. For now these military, or militant, actions were turning against the very sector of the people for whom we were claiming to be carrying out the struggle, namely the workers and the clerks, the wage-earners – whatever you call them.[7]

In this way, a diminishing number of spokesmen for the sympathizers, who basically favoured a violent change to the social-political system in the Federal Republic, were able to identify with the methods of the RAF. Very few, however, took the logical step of publicly admitting their error. Instead, they transferred their outcry from the defence of the RAF's objectives to criticism of the investigation methods of the security authorities, the way in which prosecutions were carried out and the methods of executing sentence.

LANGUAGE AS AN OPERATIONAL TOOL

The three campaign leaflets that Horst Mahler and Ulrike Meinhof published for the RAF between April 1971 and November 1972, and which accompanied and justified the first acts of violence by the Baader-Meinhof Gang, are today still the definitive framework of the strategic concept of the RAF.[8] They are embedded in a language that to a very great extent can be understood only by academically educated readers. Representatives of the worker's class cannot be motivated by this discourse. Hence, the campaign leaflets served as justification mainly *vis-à-vis* a readership comprised of intellectuals.

After the suicide of the leading members of the RAF in the Stuttgart-Stammheim prison in 1977 it became apparent that the RAF was suffering from an increasing deficit of theory. Attempts to embark upon a new theoretical discourse foundered. Such initiatives, which mainly surfaced after acts of violence, were no more than attempts to justify the attacks that had been carried out. They were endowed with the catch-phrase 'the primacy of practice'. Forward-looking ideas were not forthcoming.

From the very beginning, however, the RAF had known how to apply their catchwords to specific events and developments and consequently influence public opinion temporarily. While the names of the policemen shot by the RAF were soon forgotten, the names of the members of the RAF killed remained in the memory of the public, and above all of the sympathizers, because future operations were named after them, as 'martyrs'.

During the hunger strikes the RAF prisoners were artificially fed by the prison officers and co-opted doctors. Instead of the expression used by the government, 'artificial feeding' (*künstliche Ernaehrung*), the RAF succeeded in introducing the term 'forced-feeding' (*Zwangsernaehrung*) into public discourse. It was thereby intended to depict the state institutions as instruments of a policy that, by disregarding human rights and using force, were subjecting the RAF prisoners to treatment that could be likened to torture.

Along the same lines was the campaign against so-called 'isolation torture', which was directed against the solitary confinement of RAF prisoners. It was initiated by the members of the RAF in prison and organized by their defenders. From 1973 onwards the principal jargon expressions of this campaign were 'sensory deprivation', 'extermination imprisonment' and 'planned murder'. Thereby, the prisoners were elevated to the status of martyrs and the constitutional actions of the state branded as a 'strategy of annihilation' against the imprisoned terrorists.

In fact, there were no grounds for casting doubt on the way in which the imprisonment was conducted. The imprisoned members of the RAF were able to obtain numerous magazines, newspapers and books, to listen to the radio and records and to exercise by playing sports. They were allowed to meet for hours at a time with other inmates of the prison. They were permitted to hold almost unlimited discussions with their defence lawyers and to receive visitors. In many cases this led to accusations by other prisoners that RAF members in prisons were given preferential treatment.

In addition to agitation as an aim of the campaign, the objective was also to bring RAF members together in one prison. Self-isolation from normal prisoners on the part of the RAF terrorists by means of their extreme unfriendly behaviour led to strong group cohesion. To be sure, without such cohesion a terrorist feels lost. He is virtually forcibly directed to the group. Only the group enables him to justify his own fanatical conceptions for himself.

The campaign did in fact set into motion a surge of compassion and understanding for the situation of the prisoners. This wave of sympathy did not stop at the German borders. With the aid of left-wing groups, the lawyers of the RAF founded Committees Against Isolation Torture in the Netherlands, Belgium, France and the Scandinavian countries, in which a large number of psychologists and some doctors collaborated for quite a long time.

On 25 February 1976, the lawyer Klaus Croissant, sentenced on 16 February 1979 to a long period of imprisonment, stated at a congress of a large number of left-wing organizations in Hamburg, that the Federal Republic was the first state that permitted torture in the field of justice, and that torture had been made legal by means of a court judgement (on solitary confinement).[9] At another event in Hamburg, he said that the attitude and practices of the state with regard to the RAF prisoners could be described as 'New Fascism' and that the Third Senate of the Federal Court was 'in the tradition of the Third Reich'.[10]

In the first years of the RAF attacks the majority of lawyers who were appointed by the terrorists to conduct their defence manifested the same social-political aims as the terrorists themselves. Starting in 1972, the RAF prisoners organized a number of hunger-strike actions by means of a communication network that was set up and maintained by the lawyers. On the instructions of the Command Group, which was awaiting trial in the Stuttgart-Stammheim prison, the prisoners were to 'use their bodies as a weapon' against the state. At times, up to fifty individuals were on hunger strike. Hunger-strike actions continued into 1985.

The objective of these actions was to create political pressure to further the terrorists' demands to be incarcerated together and to generate a favourable climate for further attacks. The hunger-strike actions were accompanied by public campaigns organized by the 'legal periphery' of the terrorists in order to mobilize public opinion and to be in a position to declare any suicide resulting from hunger strike as equivalent to murder. Holger Meins, who died in November 1974 as the result of a hunger strike had written earlier:

> As I see it, a hunger strike is firstly very dangerous because it can sometimes be fatal, and secondly because then there's no going back. If I should die in prison, then it was murder – no matter what the pigs might say.[11]

In front of a Committee of Investigation after the suicides of Baader, Raspe and Ensslin, the leading members of the RAF, Irmgard Moeller was asked how she differentiated death from hunger strike. She replied, 'It's murder'.[12]

From a large number of statements on the part of the terrorists in cell-circulars, followers' letters and letters smuggled from prison cells, it is clear that hunger strikes, and also possible suicides, were to be used as weapons in the struggle against the state and the contemporary social structure. In every case, suicide in prison was to be publicized as murder and thus to be considered a pretext for further terrorist attacks.

Nevertheless, the hope that, after the liberation operation in Mogadiscu, the suicides of the RAF members imprisoned in Stammheim (Baader, Raspe and Ensslin) would become a beacon for further terrorist attacks did not materialize. There were, it is true, bombings and explosive attacks in the Federal Republic and in neighbouring countries. This was, however, only a short flare-up of violence and did not further the aims of the RAF.

After the first murders, most publications of the German print media handled the question of terrorism in the FRG with greater restraint and more objective presentation of the facts than had previously been the case. However, the propaganda ventures of the lawyers charged with the defence of the RAF prisoners induced some prominent figures to take positions which no longer corresponded with the developments, which had in the meantime taken place. Once again, making excuses for the methods and goals of the terrorists was avoided. Instead, the state and its counter-measures were denigrated. The main accusation of the publications in question was that conservative forces were using the fight against terrorism to set up a 'police and surveillance state' in the Federal Republic.

At the beginning of 1976, Heinrich Böll published a book entitled *The Lost Honour of Katarina Blum*. This told the story of a woman who gets involved in a love affair with a man without knowing he is a terrorist. The reckless reporting of a newspaper correspondent which does not stop short of the woman's intimate circle, and the foolish questioning by police officers finally lead Katharina Blum to shoot the reporter. In the foreground of the story are stupid policemen and a characterless newspaper man. In a preface, Böll says:

> The characters and the treatment of this story are imaginary. If there should emerge similarities in this account between certain journalistic practices and those of the *Bild Zeitung* [a newspaper], such similarities are neither intended nor unintentional, but unavoidable.[13]

A film was made of the book and subsequently broadcast a number of times on West German television. In the commentary to the last presentation, the announcer suggested that today Heinrich Böll would probably not have written the book and the film in quite the same way.

In May 1977, Heinrich Böll and Günter Wallraff published a book *Reports on the State of Mind*. Heinrich Böll's contribution was a satire on the investigation work of the security services in the field of terrorism. Günter Wallraff contributed a 'documentation' of investigations which, he claimed, had been conducted against him for suspicion of membership in a terrorist organization. Both pieces attempted to prove that the security services had themselves fraudulently set up the grounds for suspicion that they were investigating.[14]

Immediately after the murder of the Federal Solicitor General Siegfried Buback by the RAF on 7 April 1977 in Karlsruhe, the communist writer Ehrich Fried wrote a poem about his death. The heart of the poem consists of the following sentence:

This piece of flesh
thought it was doing justice
but did injustice.[15]

Thus, the dead man was described as a thing which had no value in and of himself. The error in his would-be philosophy of life was conceded to him. He was, on the other hand, portrayed as the willing accessory of a justice that does not recognize its own role and cannot differentiate between the interests of the social classes. Therefore, Buback, in the eyes of Fried, was only a 'part of the injustice'. Overall, the poem does not focus on the murdered man, who in his lifetime had had to prosecute murderers in order to protect the lives of human beings. Rather, the aim of the poem has been to brand the prosecution of murderers and enemies of a democratic constitution as injustice.

The student newspaper *Goettinger Nachrichten* expressed itself even more clearly. Two weeks after the murder of Siegfried Buback it published an anonymous obituary signed 'Mescalero'. It reads as follows: 'My immediate reaction, my consternation, after the shooting of Buback can be quickly portrayed: I could not, did not want to (and still do not want to) conceal my furtive delight'. The article also says:

> I regret it somewhat that we can't put a photo of this face in the small red and black album of criminals that we will publish after the Revolution, so that we might be reminded of the most sought after and most hated criminal of the world.[16]

In June 1977, forty-four professors and four lawyers published a 'documentation' on the murder of Siegfried Buback. It reprinted the Mescalero Obituary with the explanation that the right to free expression of political points of view was thereby being observed, in order to stimulate 'a rethinking about the conditions of violence in our society'. Nowhere, however, did the forty-eight authors give any indication that their opinion differed from that of the anonymous author Mescalero. The 'documentation' thus manifested understanding for the acts of the RAF by means of an intentionally inadequate analysis and by the intentional avoidance of discussion. Attached to the 'documentation' was an article by Rosa Luxemburg written in 1905 on the assassination of the Tsarist Governor General. By associating this assassination with Siegfried Buback's murder it was intended to demonstrate to the readers that the situation in the Federal Republic in 1977 was comparable to the conditions prevailing in Tsarist Russia in 1905.[17]

On 5 June 1974, in Grunewald, Berlin, a '2nd June Movement' Commando murdered the group member Ulrich Schmücker for being a 'traitor'. The Commando justified this murder with a long quotation from the RAF battle-document 'Urban Guerrilla and Class Struggle', in which capitalism is dialectically made responsible for action. On 14 April 1975 Norddeutscher Rundfunk broadcast a *Panorama* programme by Stefan Aust in which it was alleged that Ulrich Schmücker was an agent of the Verfassungsschutz, the secret service for internal security: a service which had not provided adequate protection for him.

The illustrated magazine *Stern* published two articles on 2 November 1978 and on 15 March 1979, in which it was alleged that a member of the murder squad was also an agent of the Verfassungsschutz. It was therefore, possible that 'an agent of the Verfassunsschutz had participated in the murder of a human-being'.

In another programme by Stefan Aust, *Panorama* stated on 19 June 1979 that a secret agent of the Verfassungsschutz had actually taken part in the murder of Ulrich Schmücker. The preparations for the murder had, it claimed, been known to the Verfassungsschutz. A Verfassungsschutz surveillance group had been in the vicinity of the scene of the crime and had not prevented the murder.

Propaganda help for terrorism of this kind could develop because between 1973 and 1975 the terrorists' lawyers had succeeded in building up their own agitation apparatus. In frequent speeches to New Left groups and at universities they continuously attacked the system of implementation of sentences against terrorists. The lawyer Klaus Croissant, who was arrested on 23 June 1973 and later given a conditional discharge, moved to France on 11 July 1977 and made the same accusation in interviews by French newspapers and on French television. He was arrested on 30 September 1977 in Paris and extradited to the Federal Republic on 17 November 1977.

With the arrest and subsequent sentencing of Croissant and other lawyers it was revealed that the defence lawyers had additionally set up a communication network, by means of which the orders of leading members of the RAF in jail could be transmitted to commando groups operating outside the prisons. In this connection, ten defence lawyers had not only acted as messengers, but had also smuggled weapons into the prisons that were to be kept in readiness for a planned break-out, and had themselves participated in terrorist acts as well as organized such attacks.

This knowledge, gained partly as it was in long-drawn-out court proceedings, diminished the readiness of opinion formers to stand up for the alleged rights of the terrorists. After the kidnapping of the Employers' President Hanns Martin Schleyer, there was a complete withdrawal from making statements by publicists who until then had spoken up for the 'legal treatment' of terrorists and had appealed for understanding for their motives. In the course of the kidnapping the RAF had murdered uninvolved people with unprecedented brutality, for example the driver and the three policemen designated to protect Schleyer. German television and the German press carried out the request of the Federal Government, and during the forty days' duration of the kidnapping they reported on events with extreme reserve. They published none of the communiqués or demands sent to them by the terrorists. By this the police forces gained time for their searches and the government avoided pressure from public opinion to yield to the demands of the terrorists.

THE RAF AFTER THE MURDER OF HANNS MARTIN SCHLEYER

The Federal Republic did not give in to the demands made by the RAF after the kidnapping of Hanns Martin Schleyer and the murder of his escorts. On 8 September 1977 the leader of the SPD, Willy Brandt, addressed the terrorist sympathizers in an appeal published in the media. In his proclamation he stated that the sympathizers were 'responsible for the terrible deeds to an incomparably higher degree than those fanatics who pull the trigger of the machine-gun'. Without them, the assassins would be helpless. They formed the

> backdrop of encouragement in front of which the murderers can act as heroes – must act, because without the psychic and psychological scenery life in the underground and murder cannot be sustained. They provide the nourishment, the equipment, the sanctuary, without which the terrorists could not hang on to their absurd and bloody dreams of the People's War.[18]

The German Conference of Bishops published a statement on 21 September 1977 in which it said, *inter alia:*

Numerous faculties in our high schools and universities have for many years taught and recommended theories of non-acceptance of and violence against developed industrial societies. Can one avoid the thought that the terrorists obtained their ideological armoury here and desired to translate their false and utopian theories into fact? We must ask ourselves whether perhaps certain theories of conflict that have entered into the field of education have made possible a spiritual misdirection among young people. . . . In the mass media, and even in the classroom, there were, and there are still, attempts to degrade and ridicule our state, its constitution, its laws and its representatives. . . . Frequently the concepts of justice, order and institutions have been characterized as the embodiment of the reactionary and the outdated.[19]

On 18 October 1977, a special unit of the Federal Border Guard, GSG 9, stormed the Lufthansa aircraft *Landshut* that had landed in Mogadiscu after having been hijacked by a Palestinian commando in Mallorca with a view to supporting the demands of the RAF. In the early hours of the morning of the same day, Andreas Baader, Jan Carl Raspe and Gudrun Ensslin took their own lives in the Stuttgart-Stammheim prison. On 19 October 1977 the kidnappers murdered Hanns Martin Schleyer.

In their communiqué on the murder of Hanns Martin Schleyer, the RAF immediately stated that the death of the prisoners of Stammheim had been a 'massacre'. Conforming to the old terminology, the RAF described the suicide of their leading members as murder committed by the state. Arising from this there ensued discussions, above all among factions of the New Left. The post-mortem examination of the bodies, which was carried out together with non-German scientists, and the subsequent examination by an independent committee, however, confirmed that Baader, Raspe and Ensslin had indeed taken their own lives.

The fact that the Federal Republic had not let itself be blackmailed by the terrorists and that the rescue operation of the hostages in the Lufthansa airplane was successful were seen by the 'legal periphery' and by sympathizers in general as a defeat for the RAF. It then took the RAF eighteen months to prepare for new actions. At first, these operations were unsuccessful: on 25 June 1979, members of the RAF attempted to blow up the then Supreme Commander of NATO in Europe, Alexander Haig, on his way to NATO Headquarters near Brussels; on 31 August 1981, members of the RAF carried out a bomb attack on the NATO Air Force Headquarters in Ramstein (Pfalz). Eighteen American soldiers and two German civilians were injured. On 15 September 1981 members of the RAF fired two RPG-7 rockets at the car of Frederik J.Krösen, Commanding General of the US Army in Europe. The attack failed.

These failures gave rise to the question of whether the RAF had lost their effectiveness in practice. In its theory, also, clear shortcomings had been apparent since the mid-1970s. The RAF had not been able to issue any new strategic pamphlets. Agitational assistance for the RAF until the end of 1984 was therefore confined to declarations from the 'legal periphery'. Only a few individuals in the public life, who themselves had no links to the RAF, made use of the terrorism programme to attack the investigation measures of the state, and thus state institutions at large. Others, by using the development of the RAF as a model, attempted to project from their own association with the protest movement in the 1960s into a future in which the 'Revolutionary Movement' would once again become possible.

Stefan Aust, the author of the two television programmes directed against the Verfassungsschutz, published a book on the 'Baader-Meinhof Complex'. There he explains that the plan of a handful of young people 'to destroy state dominance in specific areas' had come to terms with 'the omnipresence of the system'. The expanded security apparatus with its computer-systems and new laws passed by Parliament had led to the defeat of the RAF.[20] The author intentionally left the question open as to whether Baader, Raspe and Ensslin had committed suicide or had been murdered. His attachment to the student protest groupings was not concealed.

The writer Günter Wallraff, who during the 1970s had been in contact with members of the RAF, was informed on 28 June 1979 by the Federal Minister of the Interior that his telephone had been tapped between March and May 1974. This information, made available to him legally, was used by him for a book entitled *Akteneinsicht* ('Insight into the File'). In this book he stated that the then Federal Minister of the Interior, Dr Zimmermann, had acted after the murder of Gerold von Braunmühl as though he had 'limitless go-ahead for all the strong measures that he still had up his sleeve'. For Dr Zimmermann, the murder of von Braunmühl had been an opportunity to expand still further the 'surveillance state' and to weaken the protection of information (confidentiality). He, Wallraff, was 'not a believer in the conspiracy theory that saw terrorists as nothing more than *agents provocateurs*'. However, he said, it was known today, that 'time and again secret agents of the police and the Verfassungsschutz have not only created illegal preconditions for planned attacks, but have also taken part in them or obtained weapons and explosives'. There remained, he said, nothing more than the demand: 'Get rid of this state security!'.[21]

This reversal of standards, which lasted among left-wing intellectuals and the political forces that supported them until the beginning of the 1980s, was also evident in the case of the writer Peter-Paul Zahl. On 12 March 1976 Zahl was sentenced to a lengthy prison term as a member of a terrorist association on two charges of attempted murder. On 26 January 1980, he was awarded the Prize for Literature of the city of Bremen. In his novel – the ground for the award – Peter-Paul Zahl opposes and rejects the existing social structure.[22]

THE NEW RAF OFFENSIVE

The kidnapping of Schleyer did not bring to the RAF the success that it had desired. The outcome of this operation, due largely to the decisive stance of the Federal Government, was perceived by RAF sympathizers as a defeat. Attacks in 1979 and 1981 either failed or, in the case of the attack on the US Air Force base at Ramstein, did not produce the desired result. Consequently, the RAF tried to develop a new tactical/strategic concept, namely, the 'build-up of an anti-imperialist front in Western Europe'. This intention was expressed in a 'discussion and planning paper', found at the arrest of six central members of the RAF in underground hiding apartments in Frankfurt and Karlsruhe in July 1984.

In December 1984, the RAF launched its '84/85 Offensive'. During the first days of December the prisoners went on hunger strike. On 18 December a RAF commando attempted a bomb attack against the NATO school in Oberammergau. Fortunately, the bomb was defused in time. Had the attack turned out to be a success for the RAF, about thirty people would have perished. On 15 December the French Action Directe (AD) and the RAF published a joint communiqué 'for the unity of revolutionaries in Western Europe' in which they announced the forming of a 'United Front for the struggle against NATO imperialism'. On 25 January 1985 AD terrorists murdered the French General Rene Audran in front of his apartment in Paris. On 1 February 1985 two RAF terrorists shot the German armaments manager Dr Ernst Zimmermann in his house near Munich.

The hunger strike by the RAF members in prison and the operations at commando level were accompanied by attacks and attempted attacks from among the 'legal periphery' of the RAF. During the overall duration of the hunger strike, fifteen explosive attacks and twenty-five cases of arson occurred. Half of them were directed against military targets.

After the murder of Dr Ernst Zimmermann, the prisoners broke off their hunger strike. The RAF published a 'Declaration for Breaking Off the Hunger Strike'. In it, they opened realistically by stating that the anti-imperialist front had not yet attained the political, practical and organizational level that was necessary 'to set a limit on the state's open aim of annihilation'. The RAF maintained, however, that a 'rapid forward movement towards unity among West European guerillas and the attaining of a new quality of attack-structures' was possible.[23]

On 8 August 1985 the RAF continued their offensive. They carried out a heavy attack on the US Air Force base at the Rhein/Main Airport in Frankfurt. They exploded a car-bomb, killed two Americans and injured eleven passers-by. On 7 August, two members of the RAF had killed the American soldier Pimental, shooting him in the neck, in order to steal his identification card. Equipped with this card, the RAF infiltrated the sealed-off Air Force base.

The murder of the American soldier Pimental led to great debate, *inter alia*, in the 'legal periphery' of the RAF. At the commando level, the RAF saw itself forced to take a position on this question in a special paper. The explanation was entitled 'To Those Who Fight on Our Side' and consisted basically of RAF self-criticism.[24] Despite this evidence of the difficulties experienced in 'informing' the periphery of their actions – that is, justifying them – the RAF subsequently carried out two more murders. On 9 July 1986 they murdered the Board Member of Siemens AG, Professor Dr Karlheinz Beckurts. On 10 October 1986 they killed the Foreign Office Ministerial Director, Gerold von Braunmühl.

Media personalities not related to the RAF condemned the attacks or reported on them with reservation. The RAF enjoyed propaganda help only from their own extended circle. Nevertheless, publicity was gained in a variety of ways. During the 1984/85 hunger strike, relatives of the prisoners and some of their defence lawyers organized about sixty discussion evenings and solidarity meetings. Yet, the average attendance was about two hundred. There were about fifteen demonstrations, but only 1,000 persons took part in Hamburg, 1,500 in Berlin and 500 in Goettingen. On 10 January 1985 relatives of imprisoned RAF members and individuals from the 'legal periphery' occupied the European Parliament Information Office in Bonn. After the murders of General Audran and Dr Zimmermann, RAF sympathizers occupied the Land Office of the Green Party in Frankfurt. Interestingly the Greens did not oppose the action. Also, for a limited period the RAF succeeded in gaining considerable publicity from its left-wing fringe, using illegal radio transmitters.

On 24 January 1985 the Allgemeine Studenten Ausschuss (AStA-General Student Committee) of Bremen University issued a 'Declaration of the Hunger Strike by RAF Prisoners'. The Rector and the Academic Senate protested. The AStA opposed this protest and emphasized their support for the RAF prisoners.[25]

There was also evidence for solidarity in neighbouring countries. On 3–4 January 1985 people blockaded the Federal Republic embassy in The Hague. Others broke into the German Consulate General in Amsterdam and sprayed the walls with paint. An intercity train from Amsterdam to Munich was brought to a stop shortly after leaving the station at Amsterdam and was then sprayed with RAF slogans by thirty persons. On 8 January 1985 forty people took part in a solidarity demonstration in Paris. On 24 January 1985 RAF sympathizers occupied the offices of the International Committee of the Red Cross in Geneva.

The murder of the American soldier Edward Pimental on 7 August 1985 did, however cause, a loss of sympathy and support for the RAF. New-Left groups accused the RAF of an 'unnecessary' and counter-productive murder. After all, one could not see every GI in the Federal Republic as an enemy and, anyway, such an attitude could only make the development of a revolutionary movement more difficult.

The 'Frankfurt Congress' on 1–2 February 1986 did not result in the end of these debates. The original purpose of the meeting was a demonstration of power in support of the RAF, in which about 1,000 individuals took part. However, RAF adherents suffered a defeat since the overwhelming majority of the participants persistently condemned the brutality of the RAF attacks.

Despite this, further propaganda support for the RAF was subsequently forthcoming. On 13 June 1986 the 'Communist League'

(Kommunistischer Bund) and the 'General Student Committee' of the Technical University of Berlin organized an 'information event' on the subject 'What was Stammheim in Reality?'. The Rector of the University banned the meeting. It was then held in the High School of Economy (Fachhochschule fuer Wirtschaft) in Berlin. Christiane Ensslin, Thomas Herzog and Dirk Schneider, all relatives of the sentenced terrorists, addressed the meeting. The speakers maintained that Andreas Baader, Jan Carl Raspe and Gudrun Ensslin had not committed suicide, but had instead been murdered. Even the picture on the invitation leaflet to the meeting insinuated that the terrorists were murdered by the state organs.[26]

In September 1986, the head of an evangelical conference and student's centre in Switzerland published an obituary on the death of Ulrike Meinhof. Ulrike Meinhof had hanged herself in her cell in Stuttgart-Stammheim on 9 May 1976. In the obituary the student leader described Ulrike Meinhof's way of life and praised particularly the dead woman's 'social dedication'. While admittedly regretting that in the 'struggle' of the RAF 'human lives had to be destroyed', she went on:

> But your martyrdom was clear, still to see in the distortion of the reports, evident in the disproportionate security precautions, in the general hysteria, in the restrictions to the freedom of citizens, in the self-assured display by the state that we then saw.

To her homily, the author appended a poem, opening with the words:

> Thou, Sister
> Arisen aflame
> In my soul
> What can I call thee
> thou
> Who wanted the Heaven more blue . . .?[27]

That faction of the New Left considering itself as revolutionary, did not, however, succeed in the glorification of the dead terrorists. To be sure, it has increasingly criticized the actions by the RAF during recent years, because they overshadowed the true 'revolutionary policy' so as to make it unrecognizable. This faction of the radical left, however, did not go as far as endorsing the 'rituals of dissociation that were being practised by the Green Party and the "Old Left"'.

In April 1987, an 'Autonomous Group' from Frankfurt published a discussion paper with the title 'The Attempt to Define a New and Autonomous Anti-Imperial Policy' criticizing the murder of Pimental. It includes the following statement:

> As long as the RAF defines the Beckurts murder on the basis of the same political and ideological understanding as the Pimental execution and the Air Base attack it is for me – in terms of a political strategy – counter-revolutionary. 'Admittedly' a liquidation could be an expression of revolutionary struggle; if, however, it becomes policy in itself, it deteriorates into left-wing self-justice.

On the other hand, the paper warns against the 'legalists' who consider a 'peaceful change' of the system to be possible and wish thereby to justify the appropriate policy – that the RAF has run aground and that fifteen years of RAF militant strategy have brought no success. No matter how one criticizes the RAF, however, the paper went on, one must also remember that an anti-imperialist strategy was necessary and that armed struggle made sense because 'the collapse of the current RAF strategy does not mean for us the disarming of the armed struggle, but its rejuvenation'. That, however, could only happen and have prospects of greater success if one's own strategy was oriented 'towards evolutive processes within the mass movements'.[28]

Interestingly, the point of departure for some of the Greens towards state and government, was somewhat similar. They too wanted a different republic; besides the legal means to combat the present state and its instruments, they did not exclude violent methods. This attitude was justified by them in the argument that, in individual cases, indeed, violence might not be 'legal' but it suffices if it be 'legitimate'.[29]

The discussions about the problem of violence within the organizations of the Greens has not been settled yet.[30] This can be explained by the origins of some of the Greens. The most important wing of the 'Green-Alternative-List' in Hamburg, for instance, is an offspring from the 'Communist League', a former Maoist party. Other representatives of the Greens are former members or supporters of terrorist groups. Brigitte Heinrich, member of the 'Rainbow Faction' Member of the European Parliament since 1984, was sentenced to twenty-one months in prison on 25 July 1980 by the Law Court of Karlsruhe on the charge of having smuggled hand grenades and mines for the RAF from Switzerland into the Federal Republic. Hans Christian Stroebele, Member of Parliament in Bonn, was sentenced to ten months imprisonment by the Federal law Court on March 24, 1982, because he participated as a lawyer in setting up a communication network between the prisoners of the RAF and the activists outside the jails. One has to admit, nevertheless, that until today no new recruits of the RAF have come out of the ranks of the Greens.

TERRORISM FROM THE RIGHT

German right-wing terrorism has two roots. One is the National Democratic Party (NPD), which still is the strongest force in German right-wing extremism, at least in numbers. The NPD has experienced a continuing process of decline. This process of decay turned out to be an injection of numbers to some small Neo-Nazi groups, which were the second source of German right-wing terrorism. Young members of the NPD joined the ranks of these Neo-Nazi groups and introduced more militancy into their organization.

Neo-Nazi groups which became a hot-bed for terrorism were the 'Aktionsgemeinschaft Nationaler Sozialisten' (ANS/NA) (Action Community of National Socialists) and the 'Deutsche Aktionsgruppen' (DA) (German Action Groups). Head of this organization was the former lawyer Manfred Röder, now in jail. 'Fuehrer' of the ANS/NA was the former lieutenant of the Bundeswehr, Michael Kühnen, now also in jail.

Two other organizations of German right-wing extremism, which resorted to terrorism later, were the 'Wehrsportgruppe Hoffmann' (Military Sport Group Hoffmann) and the 'Volkssozialistische Bewegung Deutschlands/Partei der Arbeit' (VSBD/PdA) (German Socialist Peoples' Movement/Party of Labour). The Wehrsportgruppe Hoffmann has been dismantled. Hoffmann and some of his followers were sentenced to long imprisonment. The VSBD/PdA and its youth organization 'Junge Front' (Young Front) were forbidden and declared illegal by the Federal Minister of Interior on 26 January 1982. The leaders were sentenced to imprisonment.

The violent activities of Neo-Nazis which caused a bloody track through Germany during 1981 and 1982 were stopped successfully. To be sure, right-wing terrorism has never enjoyed the support of sympathizers which left-wing terrorists obtained. The Neo-Nazis attempted, it is true, the same methods of operation as the left-wingers and resorted to conspiratory conducts, but the decisive and consistent response of law enforcement and courts of justice caused heavy losses to their organizations and the draining away of their supportive environment.

In February 1983, the Kexel/Hepp Group was smashed too. The six members of this organization had raided a bank in Hesse and taken 130,000 DM as booty. They had carried out bomb attacks against the cars of American soldiers and had wounded two soldiers. Walter Kexel was suspected of having participated in an attack with explosives against a Jewish restaurant on 9 August 1982. When he was sentenced by the Frankfurt court to thirteen years' imprisonment (on 15 March 1985), he committed suicide.

In addition, the attempt by Neo-Nazis to gain allies and auxiliaries from hooligans and common criminals failed. In October 1983, Neo-Nazis from all parts of the Federal Republic – together with rockers, skin-heads and drop-outs – assembled in Berlin to break up a soccer game between Germany and Turkey. They counted on and planned a 'battle' with Turkish guest workers who were expected to come as spectators. The effective force of 3,000 policemen prevented the riot. Numerous Neo-Nazis and rowdies were arrested.

On 7 December 1983 the Federal Minister of Interior, Friedrich Zimmermann, outlawed the ANS/NA. In March of 1984 its leader Michael Kühnen fled to Switzerland and later to France. On 2 July *Stern* interviewed him in Paris. Kühnen was described as a 'Fuehrer' who had left his comrades in the lurch. The remaining members of his organization in Germany began to wonder why they should live underground when the leader in Paris enjoyed a comfortable living *à la français*. Kühnen replied to these questions with 'Letters from the Exile' stating he would reorganize the organization from his 'banishment' in France and then return to Germany in 1985. On 5 October 1984 the French authorities expelled Kühnen. On 25 January 1985 he was sentenced to imprisonment for three years and four months by the law court in Frankfurt. In addition, he has had to expect further criminal lawsuits pending in the law courts in Hamburg, Flensburg and Braunschweig.

The head of the Wehrsportgruppe Hoffmann, Karl-Heinz Hoffmann, was sentenced to nine years and six months imprisonment by the law court in Nuremberg on 30 June 1986, on the charge of leadership of a criminal association.

Right-wing terrorism is today even more marginal since it provides for no convincing strategy and ideology as was the case when it first emerged. Its followers confuse individual inclination towards violence with political engagement. To be sure, after the arrests of all the leaders able to motivate their adherents, the remaining members of the respective Neo-Nazi groups seem to be without future. Terrorism of the right does not represent a real threat for the time being.[31]

THE VIEW AHEAD

During the early phases left-wing and liberal intellectuals supported the RAF verbally. They shared the same aims as the RAF, namely the destruction of the prevailing social structure. Although they themselves did not wish to apply force, nevertheless, for a long time they sympathized with the violent acts committed by the RAF. It is only during that period that one can speak of a genuine lobby for German terrorism. In the course of the years, this propagandist support has diminished to simple agitation, emanating from the 'legal arm' of the RAF and able to address only the immediate field of the RAF.

As a matter of fact, within the New Left, the RAF today is isolated to a rather large extent. It is no longer in a position to disseminate its policy to those fragments that still exist or to justify its operations beyond its own immediate boundaries. That does not mean, however, that the RAF is incapable of carrying out any further attacks. Due to its relatively small, hard-core membership it will for the foreseeable future be in a position to recruit new fighters. Thrown back upon itself, its attacks will probably be more precipitate than previously, more unpredictable and more brutal. For the next several years the Federal Republic of Germany will have to live with RAF terrorism attacks.

There remains within the autonomous groups of the New Left a potential that continues to believe that the 'revolutionary struggle' is both necessary and possible. Since, however, their belief is that the use of force must remain as part of a mass movement, they represent no danger to public safety in the immediate future.

NOTES

1   'Revolutionaerer Zorn', 4, January 1978, p. 17.
2   Horchem, Hans Joseph, 'Terror in Europa', *Beitraege zur Konflikt-forschung*, 4, 1986, p. 36.
3   *Der Spiegel*, 3, 10 January, 1972.
4   *Kollektiv RAF – Ueber den bewaffneten Kampf in West-Europa*, Rotbuch 29, Berlin: Wagenbach Verlag, October 1971.

5   *Renato Curcio: Brief an die RAF von Dezember 1974*, translated into German, probably by an RAF member.

6   *Renato Curcio: Brief aus dem Gefaengnis von Casale Monferrato*, Milano, ABC, 9, 6 March, 1975.

7   Bäcker, Hans Jürgen and Horst Mahler, 'Die Linke und der Terrorismus, Gespräche mit Stefan Aust', *Die Linke im Rechtstaat*, Vol. 2, Berlin, 1979, p. 189

8   Meinhof, Ulrike, *Das Konzept Stadtguerilla*, April 1971; Mahler, Horst *Die Luecken der revolutionaeren Theorie schliessen – die Rote Armee aufbauen*, June 1971; Meinhof, Ulrike, *Stadtguerilla und Klassenkampf; Der Spiegel*, 18, 24 April, 1972.

9   Croissant, Klaus, 'Über die politische Bedeutung des Verfahrens gegen die RAF', Rede waehrend der Aktionstage an der Ruhr-Universitaet Bochum, 2 December, 1975.

10   Croissant, Klaus, 'Das Verbot der Befuerwortung von Gewalt und sein politischer Zusammenhang', Lecture given on 25 February 1976.

11   Binder, Sepp, *Terrorismus*, Bonn, 1978, p. 46.

12   Ibid., p. 47.

13   Böll, Heinrich, *Die verlorene Ehre der Katharina Blum*, Munich, 1986.

14   Böll, Heinrich, and Günter Wallraff, *Berichte zur Gesinnungslage*, Hamburg, 1977.

15   Fried, Ehrich, *So kam ich unter die Deutschen*, Hamburg, 1977, p. 103.

16   *Göttinger Nachrichten*, April 1977.

17   *Buback-Nachruf – Eine Dokumentation*, Berlin, 1977.

18   Quoted by Sepp Binder, op. cit., Note 11, p. 103.

19   *Dokumentation zu den Ereignissen und Entscheidungen im Zusammenhang mit der Entführung von Hanns Martin Schleyer und der Lufthansa-Maschine Landshut*, Bonn, Presse und Informationsamt der Bundesregierung, 1977, p. 45.

20   Aust, Stefan, *Der Baader-Meinhof-Komplex*, Hamburg, 1985, p. 581.

21   Wallraff, Günter, *Akteneinsicht*, Göttingen, 1987, p. 123.

22   *Kriminalistische Studien: Im Vorfeld des Terrorismus*, Vol. 3, Part 3 (Militante Gewalt), Bremen, 1986, p. 46.

23   *Zusammen kämpfen*, special edition, February 1985.

24   *Zusammen kämpfen*, January 1986.

25   *Terroristen im Kampf gegen Recht und Menschenwuerde*, Bonn, Bundesministerium des Innern, 1985, p. 18.

26   *Flugblatt des Kommunistischen Bundes und des AStA der Technischen Universität Berlin.*

27   Traitler, Reinhild, Neue Wege, September 1986, p. 248.

28   *Der Versuch, eine autonome, antiimperialistische Politik – neu – zu bestimmen*, Schwarzer Faden 23, Grafenau and *taz* 16 April 1987.

29   *Argumente, Grüne und Gewalt*, Dokumentation der CDU/CSU-Fraktion im Deutschen Bundestag, 2 January 1987; *taz* 3 June 1987.

30   *taz*, op.cit., note 29.

31   Horchem, Hans Joseph, 'Terrorismus in der Bundesrepublik Deutschland', *Beitraege zur Konfliktforschung*, 1, 1986, p. 18.

Chapter 3

Tolerating terrorism in Israel

Noemi Gal-Or

INTRODUCTION

'One man's terrorist is another man's freedom fighter' has been a statement constantly rejected by Israeli society. Recently, however, this consensus has been shattered. Change in opinion in this matter is probably one of the more important indications of the socio-psychological blurring which has grasped Israeli society. Interestingly, intellectuals, jurists, some politicians and other public figures have not, as in the past, united to counter and denounce the phenomenon of terrorism in Israel when it is perpetrated by Jews. Israeli society, which formerly so absolutely and unanimously rejected Arab terrorism, international terrorism and terrorism in general, has been definitely shocked into a state of uncertainty.

A comparison of the active engagement of factors within Israeli society endorsing Jewish-Israeli terrorism on the one hand, and Arab terrorism on the other, will reveal different patterns of attitude and behaviour. Apart from an insignificant fraction of the extreme left, overall Jewish-Israeli society is definitely opposed to any kind of Arab terrorism. Moreover, its definition for this kind of terrorism belongs to the exhaustive version rather than the narrow one.[1] Yet, when referring to Jewish terrorism, Jewish-Israeli society lays different emphases, is interested in and establishes categories of definition according to the national identity of the terrorist actors. The primary basic distinction refers to Jewish-Israeli versus Arab (Israeli and non-Israeli) terrorism. The other differentiation concerns the kinds of Jewish-Israeli terrorism. Thus, the support for the so-called 'Jewish Underground' is undoubtedly overwhelming when compared to the indifference characterizing the attitude towards other terrorists, such as the TNT group, the Lifta gang and individuals who resorted to counter-Palestinian terrorism.

Pro-terrorist lobbies were, indeed, quite rare in the 1960s and 1970s. The terrorist support network surfaced only with the disclosure of the Jewish Underground. This novelty has actually awakened our interest in the pro-terrorist lobbying phenomenon as a characteristic of liberal democratic and pluralist societies. A comparison of pro-Arab and pro-Jewish terrorism lobbies entails the analysis of two different populations. Due to obvious political reasons, pro-Arab terrorism lobbies within Israel have been significantly less active, than the opposite case, indeed, hardly existent. Arab or Palestinian terrorists[2] could have counted on silent consent from the Arab population in the Territories and, to a growing degree, within the 'green' (international) borders of the state of Israel, in addition to a very limited logistical support. Jewish supporters of Arab terrorists are an exception; only two lawyers in favour of the Palestinian struggle for self-definition have regularly supported, albeit within the framework of legal limits, persons accused of being terrorists. The decisive pro-Arab/Palestinian terrorism lobby is larger, but it operates outside Israeli society and outside the country's territory. This lobby is comprised particularly of the Palestinian organizations and the Arab terrorism-supporting states. Various pro-Palestinian (leftist or rightist) organizations, private and public, all around the globe do actually act as pro-terrorist lobbies as well.

Palestinian and Jewish-Israeli terrorism: an overview

The history of Jewish and Arab societies in Palestine, and later in Israel, is shaded by continuous terrorist activity. While there have been periods of relative relaxation, other times have witnessed intensive lethal violence. The Arab–Israeli conflict has its roots in the Arab–Jewish struggle for dominance of the same piece of land – the Land of Israel, or Palestine. In modern history, this can be traced back to the early years of the twentieth century. Several significant waves of Arab terrorism against Jewish settlers marked the pre-state period: the violent events of 1921, 1922 and 1929 and those during the Arab Revolt of 1936–9[3] in which there were numerous terrorist attacks on life and property (but also against British installations). The Jews were not slow to respond and three underground organizations were established within the Jewish community: the Hagana, the IZL and the LEHI, the latter two of which also used terrorist methods in their struggle against their Arab and British enemies.

Violence continued to characterize the Arab–Jewish relationship after the foundation of the state of Israel. Arab (Palestinian) terrorists used to carry out assaults against Israelis from across the borders, infiltrating the country, often with the connivance and sometimes with the active support of the neighbouring Arab countries. However, Palestinian terrorism received an enormous impetus after the Six Days War of 1967 and spilled over from anti-Israeli terrorism within Israel, including the Territories, to assaults abroad, mainly in Europe. The international terrorist attacks were aimed at dragging foreign powers into the conflict and manipulating intervention in favour of the Palestinian cause, and also to bring international influence to bear on Israeli policy by targeting non-Israeli, particularly west European, goals.

To be sure, Jewish-Israeli terrorism has developed differently. Compared with Arab terrorism it was far less significant. It managed to last only a few years during the early 1950s and was not directed against the Arab–Israeli population (it concentrated on internal Jewish-Israeli issues instead).[4] The long intermission in Jewish terrorist activity lasted until 1980, which marked the surprising revival of this violent behaviour within Jewish-Israeli society. Only in 1984 did it become evident that the spectacular terrorist assaults against notorious Palestinian figures were perpetrated by Jewish terrorists. Although these were not the first incidents of Jewish terrorism to take place in the 1980s the exposure of the Jewish Underground marked the advent of a creeping pro-terrorist legitimation.

Two main characteristics distinguish Jewish from Palestinian terrorism: First, Palestinian terrorism has always been primarily directed against the Jewish-Israeli population, and motivated by the desire to destroy the Israeli state. It should, therefore, be defined as anti-state and anti-regime terrorism as well. Jewish-Israeli terrorism, on the other hand, was not at all times anti-Arab. Sometimes, instead, it was of the anti-regime type and of a protesting nature. Nevertheless, our study will refer to the late appearances of Jewish terrorism, which, while typically anti-Palestinian, are not anti-state, anti-Israel or even anti-regime as such. Rather, Jewish terrorists have perceived their actions not as opposition to the state or government, but instead as support for the authorities (ideologically more close to them than any previous Israeli government) in completion of their duties (securing the safety of the settlers and preventing the establishment of a sovereign Palestinian state).

Second, the ground nurturing Palestinian terrorism differs from the supportive environment of Jewish terrorism. Palestinian terrorism depends upon the assistance of sympathetic Arab states which are hostile to Israel (therefore, Palestinian terrorism is also state-supported terrorism) and upon pro-Palestinian elements within non-Arab societies sympathizing with the Palestinian cause. Jewish-Israeli terrorism may count mainly on support from specific segments of Israeli society. However, it also enjoys foreign assistance based almost entirely in Jewish groups within the USA.

These differences between the two kinds of terrorism have important consequences for the efforts of the Israeli government to counter either kind of terrorism. While attempts to reduce and limit the volume of pro-Jewish terrorism lobbying require initiative within the realm of domestic policy, parallel efforts against pro-Arab terrorism lobbies have had necessarily to focus also on the domain of foreign policy. In view of the stability and integrity of democracy, it might sometimes have been even more important to influence local public opinion and the general atmosphere prevailing within the country rather than to operate on the foreign relations arena.

PRO-PALESTINIAN TERRORISM LOBBIES

The pro-Palestinian terrorism lobbies can be classified according to three categories: (a) lobbies within Israel; (b) the PLO and the Arab world; and (c) elements on the international scene.

Palestinian terrorism supporters within Israel

Individuals actively and overtly favouring the Palestinian 'armed struggle' are predominantly Israeli Jews. Until the December 1987 developments of the popular unrest, sympathizing with hostile Palestinian elements within Israel would have undermined the delicate equilibrium prevailing in the Jewish–Arab relations of the citizens. Clearly, as a consequence of the nature of the conflict, the Arab population has been from the onset the primary subject of the authorities' vigilance in matters of security. On the other hand, from the Arab-Israeli point of view, there has been the constant tension of conflicting loyalties. Belonging to the Palestinian ethnic group conflicts with loyalty to one's citizenship. This paradox – combining commitment to conform and resistant separatism – has provided the incentive to act overtly in favour of one's national brethren who are one's states' enemies. Indeed, Israeli Jews, more than Israeli Arabs, can therefore better perform a supporting role. The few examples of this belong to the ideological extreme left wing of society, to its Soviet-Communist oriented flank.

Two Jewish-Israeli lawyers have dedicated themselves to safeguard and care for the respect of human rights of Palestinians and to advocate (in some cases) for Palestinians suspected of terrorism. Their efforts have not been restricted to representation in trial only, but expand also to cover the international forums. Lea Zemel and, in particular, Felicia Langer are well-known for their fight for the human rights of the Palestinians. Langer, activist in the former MKI (Israeli Communist Party) in the 1950s, joined, after the split in the party, the new RKH (New Communist List) party, the electorate of which comes overwhelmingly from among the Arab population.[5] Participating in international conferences and initiatives abroad relevant to the Palestinian struggle for self-determination, she is complementing her legal supportive efforts. While morally and socially sustained by human rights organizations from abroad, these two lawyers are rather isolated within Jewish-Israeli society.

Usually, organizations, groups and institutions too open and articulate in their endorsement of the Palestinian national self-determination aspirations, and ambivalent towards the strategy of 'armed struggle', have been declared by Israeli authorities as terrorist supportive elements. The Jewish-Palestinian Centre for Alternative Information was accused of having operated as an administrative and propagandist arm for George Habash's Popular Front for the Liberation of Palestine (PFLP). The centre was established to serve a lobby, influencing public opinion by way of supplying information concerning the Israeli rule in the Territories, focusing especially on human rights. It has operated as an alternative source of information, parallel to the official Israeli channel. The people involved in this activity formed a small group (Mazpen) consisting of extreme left veterans of the 1960s (the centre's director, Michael Warshavsky, is Lea Zemel's husband). A significant number of its members emigrated from Israel in the late 1960s and early 1970s. They continue to operate from abroad, disseminating information and directing tourists to the Centre. One of the employees of the Centre was Ali Jaada, a terrorist who participated in an assault in the city centre of Jerusalem and was set free in the exchange deal with Ahmed Jibril's Popular Front for the Liberation of Palestine – General Command (PFLP–GC).[6] Small *ad hoc* groups, organizing to protect human rights in the Territories (not necessarily terrorists' 'rights') have been numerous. Such, for example, was the Committee Against the Strong Hand in the Territories, which has compelled the authorities to investigate the circumstances leading to the deaths of a number of Palestinians.[7]

Another development in this area was the closing down of the Jewish-Palestinian fortnightly publication *Derech Hanitzoz* (The Way of the Spark), the editors being suspected of collaboration with Nauif Hawatmeh's terrorist Democratic Front for the Liberation of Palestine (DFLP).[8] The newspaper first appeared as a monthly in 1982 circulating in leftist circles and later, in 1985, appearing every two weeks. It received indispensable material assistance more from international organizations than from domestic sources. It was known for its credibility, in particular concerning the Territories and the situation of the Palestinians. Many scandalous affairs were first disclosed by this newspaper, which served, indeed, as a pool of information for the institutionalized media. It was published in Hebrew and Arabic and had many subscribers among journalists and the intelligentsia.

An additional initiative, though not pro-terrorist, was the Palestinian Centre for the Study of Non-Violence, created and directed by a self-declared Palestinian (American Citizen) pacifist, Muhammed Awad, who did not reject Palestinian violence although he personally opted to preach in favour of the strategy of passive resistance and civil disobedience. His office was closed down in 1987 by the authorities and Awad was put under administrative custody, his deportation required (and carried out) by the government.[9]

In cases of violation of human and civil rights, the (Jewish) Israeli Association for Civil Rights and its Arab counterpart 'El Khak' have also intervened and fulfilled the role of the watchdog of democracy and safeguard of human rights.

A public opinion poll within the Palestinian population of the Territories showed that the majority of the people have endorsed the use of terrorism to further their national and political goals. This unique and exceptional survey was carried out by the American newspaper *Newsday*, the Australian television network ABC and the East-Jerusalem newspaper *Al-Fajer* in 1986. Of those interviewed, 78 per cent supported the use of violence as a justified and legitimate means to solve the Palestinian problem. They also justified the murderous assault on the bus by terrorists on the coastal highway in 1978. Sixty per cent supported the hiding of explosives in El-Al aircraft. Yassir Arafat, the leader of the PLO, was perceived by 93.5 per cent as their only legitimate representative. The survey also revealed that the higher the level of education, the greater the support for the more extremist Palestinian organizations. The results and conclusions of this poll were not accepted as representative by most of the Israeli experts on the grounds of methodological shortcomings. The questions were biased, it was argued, the interviewers were threatening youngsters, members of the youth organization of the PLO, and the editor of the survey was himself an extremist Fatah activist. Nevertheless, it was agreed by all that the survey did indeed reflect pro-terrorist tendencies in the Palestinian public.[10]

Both Arab political parties – Hadash (formerly Rakach) and the Progressive List for Freedom – have naturally endorsed the Palestinian demand for self-determination. Yet, being Israeli political parties, they have had, after all, to prove their loyalty to the state and refrain from such declarations, not to mention deeds, which could be interpreted as supporting terrorism. Any attempts – either by an organization or by an individual – in support of Palestinian terrorists could have been outlawed on charges of harassment, assisting the country's enemy, threatening the state's security, or treason.

Nevertheless, as reflected by the *de facto* situation, the imprisoned Palestinian terrorists have known rather well how to care for themselves, regardless of the lack of institutionalized support and legal backbone. This has become clearly evident in their organization within the prisons and success in maintaining a strong leadership, which fulfils the functions of judges, responsibility for education, food and the supply of luxuries, as well as representing all the Palestinian prisoners in their contacts with the prison administration. They have, furthermore, succeeded in maintaining contacts with the external environment, thanks not only to the help of the ICRC (International Committee of the Red Cross) but also due to their independent initiative (for example by transforming radios into wireless receivers to receive broadcasts transmitted from vehicles passing near the prison).[11] This kind of organization, based primarily on a reciprocal flow of information, has undoubtedly had a significant propaganda effect on outside sympathizing circles, through either the contacts kept with the prisoners or the 'multiplier effect' disseminated by released terrorists.

The PLO and the Arab world

First in importance is the natural advocate for the Palestinian terrorists, namely the Palestinian Liberation Organization (PLO). The PLO is a declared terrorist organization under Israeli law. It is the umbrella organization of all militant Palestinian organizations, thus foremost and in addition to its being a political movement it has for long been a paramilitary organization. An aggregate of various Palestinian terrorist organizations, the PLO has been mediating between its various components and 'parliamentarily' responsible for the planning and the carrying out of Palestinian terrorist assaults. Like an army (though irregular), the Palestinian Liberation Army (PLA) is also responsible for its warriors. The function of recruitment into the PLA and the education and motivation of future guerrillas and terrorists, must hence be completed by the moral and active support for the apprehended individuals. It is different from a state's regular army in that its members are not its nationals and its camps and bases are not stationed on territory governed sovereignly by the organization. Therefore, not only does the PLO's declared terrorist 'armed struggle' consist of a method of warfare forbidden by the law of war and the law of human rights, moreover, the PLO is prevented from caring for its combatants by the means of communication commonly applied in the relations among states. In other words, the PLO cannot ask for extradition, nor for pardon or amnesty; it is deprived in most cases of the right of formal visits by its representatives to terrorists imprisoned in Israeli or other prisons and cannot establish any direct and official contact with them. Not really enjoying the status of a state, acting in breach of domestic and international law and declared in Israel as a terrorist organization, this huge institution is prevented from directly, legally or politically looking after its imprisoned members or members awaiting trial. It must, therefore, look for other channels through which to respond to the imperative commitment to its people. The two options open to it are illegal activity and activity through intermediaries and undeclared emissaries.

Illegality and subversive activity in looking after its apprehended members is a typical characteristic of PLO activity. Numerous terrorist acts carried out by organizations within the PLO have been aimed, either in addition to or especially at the release of Palestinian terrorists from prison.[12] Almost all terrorist negotiation attacks have been directed precisely to achieve this purpose.[13] This has reduced the inclination of the Israeli security forces to catch the terrorists alive during violent encounters and when not needed for intelligence purposes. The fewer terrorists that are captured and imprisoned, the fewer terrorist acts of reprisal there will be for the release of the apprehended fellow terrorists. Applying extortion to free terrorists imprisoned in Israel failed to achieve the expected results until 1978. In contrast, this policy of the PLO has proved to be effectively applied on the European continent. In most cases involving the arrest of Palestinian terrorists, west European governments have preferred to get rid of the terrorists, in order to prevent future reprisals and in the mistaken belief that this policy will silence and calm Palestinian terrorist activity on their territory and against their nationals and interests. Instead of extraditing Palestinian terrorists or prosecuting them, European governments have preferred the more politically expedient alternative of expulsion.[14]

The rise in Palestinian and Arab terrorist activity in the west, in particular state-sponsored terrorism, i.e. the rude infringement of the sovereignty of leading western European states such as the United Kingdom, France and the Federal Republic of Germany, has, in the mid to late 1980s, driven the respective governments to stiffen their attitude towards foreign, non-domestic terrorism as well. Examples are the cases of Hindawi, Abdallah and Hamadi.[15] In all three cases, governments did not surrender (at least, not directly) to demands for exchanges of kidnapped nationals in the Middle-East (Lebanon) for convicted terrorists in Europe. Exchange deals switched over to other channels, using the mediation efforts of governments (in particular Syria), and buying with money and not persons (terrorists) the freedom of European hostages.[16] Seen from the perspective of the European governments, this was clearly one step forward in their fight against terrorism. State-sponsored terrorism has an address (the governments of Syria and Libya, for instance) which can be held responsible and put under pressure to break the vicious terrorist cycle. Indeed, western governments have seemed to enjoy the possibility of more effectively exerting anti-terrorist sanctions, an alternative which is denied to them when challenged by the non-state 'remote controlled' terrorist organization, for example Al-Fatah and others, which are not directly monitored by governments.

Stubborn Israeli resistance to terrorist blackmail lasted until 1978, when the first crack appeared in the wall. For the first time an Israeli government gave up the principle of non-negotiation with terrorists, consenting to exchange Palestinian terrorists for one Israeli soldier captive with the PLO. The most impressive case, however, was the exchange bargain with Ahmed Jibril (PFLP–GC) in 1985. Three Israeli soldiers held captive by Jibril's forces were returned to Israel for a 'ransom' of 1,150 Palestinian terrorists.[17] Some of these terrorists were convicted criminals serving life sentences; for others trial was still pending. Moreover, terrorists were allowed to choose their place of destination. Many preferred to return home to the Territories and Israel and some later perpetrated further terrorist attacks.

This affair raised strong emotions and objections within Israel. Apart from moral and political criticism of the government, legal criticism was raised as well. Not only was it illegal to bargain with terrorists perceived as international criminals; but, moreover, 'bending' and breaching judicial procedures to satisfy political needs seemed to be unacceptable to any democratic regime whatsoever. Unfortunately, this event coincided with another terrorist affair (those days in Israel were very delicate), the trial of the Israeli terrorist Jewish Underground. It therefore, had repercussions not only in respect to Israeli strategy against Palestinian terrorism, but far more importantly, concerning the Israeli policy of combating terrorism in general and indigenous, 'home-made', Jewish anti-Palestinian terrorism in particular. Thus, the exchange deal with Jibril was brilliantly manoeuvred to underscore the importance and competence of the PLO and, moreover, to demonstrate the organization's (in particular PFLP-GC's) concern for its members.

As already noted, the PLO is inhibited from directly lobbying for its members through the usual channels of Israeli public life. In addition to the terrorist alternative, another answer to this impotence has been to act through intermediaries and emissaries. First in this category are the Arab states. Indeed, there are two cardinal reasons why Arab states, some of them in particular, should undertake this role.

First, many PLO warriors are legally the citizens of various Arab states, in particular Jordan. They consequently enjoy the prerogative of applying to their national governments, competent and entitled by national and international law to represent them and intervene in their favour with another state. This advantage was exploited in relations with states, other than Israel, with which the Arab states maintain peaceful relations, in particular concerning those nationals arrested in western Europe. In the 1970s, indirect intervention instead of local procedures characterized Arab states' behaviour. Afraid of being dragged into the circle of violence and identifying with the Palestinian cause, Arab states exerted political and especially economic influence to achieve the release of the terrorists in Europe. This was most successful during the era of the oil crisis, which has nevertheless, meanwhile partially lost its effectiveness.[18]

Indeed, until 1967 and the Israeli occupation of the West Bank and the Gaza Strip (populated by Palestinians), Jordan, Egypt and Syria fully sustained the 'armed struggle' of the Palestinians. Their interests in annoying Israel coincided with the Palestinian interest, with the same goal of the dissolution of the state of Israel. As a matter of fact, the Palestinian terrorist commandos of the 1950s and the early 1960s were to a certain extent mercenaries of the Arab states. This was one of the reasons Israel engaged in the Sinai War of 1956 – to stop terrorism operating from the Egyptian border. Arab support of Palestinian terrorism perpetrated from their territory continued after the Six Day War. Jordan was so deeply dominated by the terrorists' involvement that it had to violently expel the Palestinians in 1970 (Black September) in order to escape the 'boomerang effect' of terrorism, which had attained threatening dimensions. Jordan's successor in supporting and hosting anti-Israeli Palestinian terrorism has been Syria, from its southern border (the so-called Fatah-Land), and since 1972 from the Lebanon.[19]

It goes without saying that the Arab states have supported the national Palestinian movement politically, in making it an issue in their foreign policy and within international organizations. Moreover, apart from diplomatic support, Arab states (like Saudi-Arabia, for instance) have heavily contributed to support the organization financially. Other governments (not only Arab governments) have provided training and other military facilities.[20]

To be sure, the Arab governments involved in the support of terrorism form an integral part of the Third World and cannot be considered as western liberal democracies. Hence, the effect of their policies with regard to terrorism are relevant to our analysis only in so far as they have initiated reaction within the western democracies targeted by this terrorism.

Elements on the international scene

The international arena offers the availability of a plentitude of organizations devoted to the idea of the human rights of individuals and nations. In this environment, within international organizations, the PLO has been able to act either directly and unilaterally or in collaboration with Arab and non-Arab states, in particular, the Eastern bloc and the non-aligned states.

The PLO and the Arab League

The PLO has consistently worked to strengthen its position within the Arab world. The means used have been primarily of a diplomatic nature (with a slight terrorist threat 'in the back of the mind'), an everlasting campaign to foster the organization's status within the Arab world. The Palestinian claim for self-determination was endorsed in 1948–9, albeit half-heartedly, by the newly created Arab League. The league failed to sustain its efforts towards Palestinian independence, however, the member states withdrawing from their position and realigning with the Cis-Jordanian monarch to enable the conquest of the part of Palestine which, according to the UN partition resolution 181 (1947), was to have become an independent Palestinian state.[21] Among the later results of the Arab League's calculated support was the legitimization of the Palestinian struggle for self-determination, including the means applied, that is the armed struggle consisting of terrorism. The Arab League has projected its support for Palestinian interests within other international forums, for example the UN, when it is there as a single, regional body. It has contented itself with verbal commitment and support only. More active engagement could not be expected from this internally split organization.

The PLO and the UN

The PLO and the Arab World can be proud of a number of significant achievements concerning the Palestinian struggle. First is the fact that the Palestinian case has become a permanent issue on the UN General Assembly's agenda. It would not be an exaggeration to claim that terrorism was the determinant reason for the institutionalization of the Palestinian case within the most important international organization. The UN's work concerning the Palestinian problem has benefited from the versatility of UN activities. Within the Assembly, the issue has been dealt with on a political declaratory level. The various resolutions referring on the one hand to the legitimation and justification of the Palestinian right for self-determination and on the other, as a complementary tactic, with the condemnation of Israeli aggression, breach of laws and violation of human rights against the Palestinian people, have served as a warhead for comprehensive efforts towards the legitimation and quasi-legalization of the Palestinian struggle.[22] The work of the various special UN Assembly's organs, in particular the Sixth Committee and the Legal Commission, testify to this. The Arab countries, in co-ordination with the communist governments and the non-aligned bloc, have been the loudspeaker for the terrorists, serving as intermediaries for the PLO regarding the right of self-determination but also endorsing the terrorist strategy as a legitimate tool in achieving it. This attitude has been most strongly reflected by a reluctance to condemn Palestinian terrorism. In fact, the lobbying efforts have diverted the UN discussions on terrorism towards perceiving the terrorists as the genuine victims of aggression rather than the true aggressors. Such lobbying has omitted the other inevitable angle, namely, considering terrorism according to the laws of war. The UN's response to Palestinian terrorism lobbying has indeed affected Israel's dual attitude to terrorism. Long years of attrition and isolation in the forefront of an anti-terrorism campaign have resulted in a selective attitude of tolerance to certain kinds of terrorism and intolerance to others.

The PLO, the European Community and the Council of Europe

Among the regional international organizations, the Organization of American States (OAS), the Organization of East and South Asia (OEAS) and the Organization of African States (OAS), have been lobbied on the Palestinian problem. Lobbying there, however, meant working on the fringes of the western world. Efforts to promote such lobbying have been easier than in western countries, since Palestinian terrorism was not inflicted on them. Moreover, support from this environment has consisted purely of governmental decision, due to the less active mechanisms of public opinion compared to the western countries. Furthermore, these organizations are weaker in their international influence than the wealthy European regional organizations, which represent the decisive portion of the industrialized world. Hence, it has been European organizations which have become more vulnerable to Palestinian terrorism, their nationals being too often victims of the Palestinian struggle for self-determination. The PLO itself has not enjoyed any representative status within either of the largest European bodies, the EC and the Council of Europe. It has therefore had to rely on the efforts of Arab governments, partners to the exchange of opinions taking place in the framework of the organizations' foreign policy. The issue of terrorism, though not permanent on the agenda of these organizations, has nevertheless been present and the attitude and reaction of the organized European states to Palestinian terrorism has been overwhelmingly negative and hostile. In contrast to the frequent surrender of individual governments to Palestinian terrorist blackmail (controlled tolerance), the organizations (and the world summits of the industrialized countries) have formally clearly objected to terrorism (including Palestinian terrorism, though not explicitly declaring so). While this stance reflects their interest (and ethics) in stopping terrorism as such, it does, however, assist in delegitimizing Palestinian terrorism in particular.

From the Palestinian point of view, terrorism has indeed put the Palestinian question on the international agenda. The most important achievement in the Palestinian interest has been the propagation of an underdog image, which has succeeded in neutralizing the negative by-products of terrorism. The pitiful image of a poor, oppressed and dispersed people has frequently been used to legitimize their leaders' choice of whatever means they find fit to bring their grievances to an end. In other words, a sophisticated measure of terrorist methods combined with a propaganda campaign has succeeded in gaining the world's sympathy; in parallel, it has reduced sympathy for Israel, which has been accused of aggression and oppression (and greater intolerance of terrorism). Briefly, terrorism has definitely proved to be a profitable strategy on the western world's arena as well. While not influencing the fate of the terrorists imprisoned in Israel, it has nevertheless been effective in lobbying for the release of Palestinian terrorists held in other countries.[23] It has also been effective in preparing the infrastructure for Palestinian anti-Israeli and anti-Jewish terrorist activity abroad, European Palestinian terrorism being the evidence.[24]

International organizations have sometimes been manipulated by nationalist terrorists to serve as the stages for legitimization. In this context, they have also exerted influence by supporting individual Palestinian terrorists at the practical level. This assistance has been carried out through work intended mainly to further and protect human rights. UN and European delegations have occasionally visited the Territories and have maintained contacts with local Palestinian notables and public figures, acting as watch-dogs of the human rights of the terrorists, both detained and imprisoned. Since each delegation has been of different composition – European parliamentarians, EC commissioners and UN specialized agencies and Assembly committee members – they have indeed covered a broad range of institutional interests. In this way, the Palestinian issue, including the care of Palestinian terrorists, has gained extensive attention.

This kind of control has been additionally carried out by other national NGOs. Two important agents concerned with the fate of the Palestinian terrorists are Amnesty International (AI) and the ICRC, which have been keeping track of the situation of the Palestinian people in the Territories, including the application of laws of human rights relevant to terrorists.[25] This kind of care has often served as an important vehicle for Palestinian lobbying in matters of terrorism. The use of so-called 'environmental' or collective punishment by the Israeli authorities has been an important factor in the growing deterioration of the Israeli image in the world and has furthered the political legitimation of the Palestinians which was initiated by terrorism. In contrast to the governmental organizations, NGO's involvement has been apolitical and less abstract, more immediate and direct. Consequently, the results have been real, experienced 'in field' and not declaratory only. They have enhanced the propagandist campaign precisely because they have delivered simple and clear messages.

Public, non-governmental bilateral friendship links between European and Arab countries have been a supplementary channel used to further the Palestinian issue. In this case, too, the PLO or Palestinian interests have been represented by the mediation of Arab states. The German–Arab friendship organization is an outstanding example of such lively co-operation. Apparently, when it comes to terrorism, this sort of mutual understanding turns out to have its particular benefits of securing Germany from becoming the victim of Palestinian terrorism as well as isolating indigenous from exogenous terrorism. Since NGOs are forums less restrained by calculations of internal and electoral domestic political pressure than governments or political parties, they have been more free to address the overall public, and express a higher degree of tolerance for terrorism in operating as tools in the formation of public opinion.

In this section I have discussed two cardinal goals of pro-Palestinian support: caring for the apprehended terrorists and the linkage between the Palestinian issue and the methods applied to further it. Achieving both goals depends upon success in creating a positive atmosphere, sympathetic with the Palestinian interests. As a matter of fact, the legitimation of terrorist activity and of the Palestinian problem, has too often led to the blurring of the boundary between terrorists and those who are not terrorists. The legitimation of the cause, by attracting world attention through terrorism, has contributed to at least a tolerance of Palestinian terrorism, if not the legitimation of terrorism as such. Yet, when it comes to active support, the Palestinians have to be content with distant, foreign and international support, albeit intensive and wide-ranging, yet minimal within Israel and the Territories.

LOBBIES SUPPORTING JEWISH-ISRAELI TERRORISM

Though Jewish-Israeli terrorism is not an original invention of the Jewish Underground uncovered in 1984, terrorism perpetrated by Israeli Jews has been rather a novelty on the Israeli political scene. Two famous Jewish terrorist organizations were active under the British mandatory rule in Palestine. Then, Jewish society disapproved, denounced terrorism and the terrorist attacks both on the grounds of moral rejection and political disagreement, stressing the counter-productivity of terrorism in Israel's struggle for national self-determination.[26] At a certain stage (1944–5), the Hagana, the largest Jewish para-military organization, enjoying the widest popularity in the Jewish community of Palestine, even co-operated with the British authorities against the IZL and LEHI combatants (a period known in the underground jargon as the hunting-time 'Saison').

The first years following the independence of the new state of Israel were used to institutionalize the pre-statehood governing apparatus and the country enjoyed a short intermission in Jewish terrorist activity in Israel. However, in 1952, a new wave of terrorism, less intensive though, reappeared on the Israeli scene. While previous terrorist assaults were launched at foreign targets (British and Arab institutions and persons), this time the enemy of the terrorist was only seldom non-Israeli. Most of the attempts were related to internal debates within Israeli society, concerning either ideological–ethical issues, social questions or items on the political agenda. The victims were therefore Jewish and Israeli citizens. Despite the differences in goals and victims, the phenomenon was rightly seen as a hangover from the pre-statehood period, the inevitable death-rattles of a group of people during the transitional state-building period. To be sure, from 1958 until early 1980, there was no terrorist activity by Jewish Israelis within Israel or the Territories.

Since 1980 five terrorist attempts, later attributed to the Jewish Underground, were perpetrated against the Palestinian population in the West Bank and Jerusalem. These were the assaults in 1980-4 on the heads of West-Bank city councils and leaders of the Palestinian National Directive Committee on the West Bank; the murderous assaults at the Islamic College and the football yard in Hebron; the attempt at the mosques in Hebron and two planned assaults that did not materialize: one to blow up the mosques on Temple Mount, the other to trap five public buses transporting Palestinians, the explosion of which was avoided at the last moment. Although there had already been several attempts against Palestinians (at non-Jewish targets such as churches, and even at Jewish opponents of the Right such as the leftist newspaper *Al Hamishmar*), at the time terrorism caught Israeli society by surprise. Furthermore, another novelty in the Israeli environment was public reaction, which overwhelmingly sympathized with the terrorists and greatly approved of at least one of its assaults (against the leaders).

Israeli society has consistently objected to and denounced terrorism in all its forms. Israeli politicians have declared it an enemy to be fought to the very end, to its annihilation. This resolute and steadfast attitude has been for long characteristic of the standing of Israeli society and politicians with regard to terrorism, based naturally on the intense experience of Arab and Palestinian terrorism. Thus, in 1980, when the first attempt at the leaders of the Palestinian National Directive Committee occurred, the rejoicing of a significant part of Israeli society (though the identity of the perpetrators remained anonymous for four years), marked an important turning point in Israel's stance against terrorism. This reaction received reinforcement when the identity of the terrorists, members of the nationalist-messianic settlers' organization in the Territories (Gush Emunim), was made public. Indeed, a fundamental moral shift in Israeli perception and attitude towards terrorism has taken place. The determined and unshaken conviction as to the evil of terrorism (*mala in se*) was undermined by the distinction between bad terrorists, who are Palestinians and others, and good, or at least just, terrorists who are the Jewish ones (predominantly though, members of the Jewish Underground, since other Jewish terrorists like Ben-Shimol, the TNT members, the Lifta gang, etc., passed almost unnoticed by an indifferent public).

The reasons and the setting for the resurgence of Jewish terrorism are elaborated elsewhere.[27] We will therefore be content here to outline the reasons for the shift in the moral attitude towards terrorism. These derive from two main sources. One is the effect of the development and expansion of nationalist elements within Israeli society after 1967 (the era after the Six Days War) and, in particular, the impact of the Gush Emunim movement. This movement, carrying the ideology of the greater land of Israel, the biblical and messianic vision of the Kingdom of Israel expanding from the Mediterranean to the Eupherat and from Lebanon to (and including) the Sinai peninsula, captured the souls and imagination of many Israelis. To implement and realize its ideology, Gush Emunim became intensively active in settling the West Bank, the Golan Heights and the district around the Gaza Strip (in particular during the Likud rule).[28] Since the new Jewish terrorism originated from this socio-ideological source it has also enjoyed its moral support.

The second reason for the change in attitude towards terrorism belongs to the realm of politics – either as a variable dependent upon ideology or as an independent variable. The ever-growing activity of Palestinian terrorists within Israel and the Territories, but also abroad in the guise of international terrorism and the Arab states' aggression culminating in the Yom-Kippur War (1973), has cultivated an increasing hostility towards both Palestinians and Arabs and pressure for revenge. The peace treaty with Egypt, stipulating withdrawal from the Sinai peninsula and the abandonment of the settlements and city of Yamit; the famous 'linkage' of the Palestinian problem and the prospects for Palestinian autonomy; and the set-backs in the normalization process with Egypt have added fuel to a rising feeling of national humiliation and disappointment concerning the political achievements of the government. Moreover, despite the peace treaty, Israel has become ever more isolated within the international family of nations. Frustration (though not immediately admitted) due to the failure and misdirection of the Lebanon war, has contributed to the false recognition that only additional extremism in the form of violence is the language understood by the enemy. The Jewish Underground (more so than the other Jewish-Israeli terrorists) has made a determined bid to symbolically fill out the vacuum created by the indecisiveness of the government. The Lebanon War has further contributed to the moral shift in Israeli society. Moral values have been eroded and sensitivity blunted by the bitter experience of a war in the midst of a civilian population and by encountering the violence, corruption and feud dominating Lebanese society. If this is the language understood by Arabs, common sense deduction argues, let us profit from it in our struggle against them. Tolerating the Jewish Underground cannot be explained separately from these political circumstances. Nevertheless, a better understanding of the dynamics steering sympathy towards the terrorists into active pro-terrorist lobbying will be gained by systematically studying the various frameworks wherein this lobbying was formed.

Governmental lobbying

The 1977 elections (resulting in the undermining of the dominant Labour Party's power for the first time and its replacement by the nationalist Herut Party and Likud Block) marked an important personnel change in the composition of the government. For the first time in Israeli history (except for a short exceptional episode in 1967), veterans of the pre-state terrorist underground became members of the ruling government and held cabinet ministries. Prime Minister Menachem Begin had been the chief commander of the IZL, the largest Jewish terrorist organization during the British mandatory rule, and Itzhak Shamir, his Foreign Minister and later Prime Minister, was operation commander of the smaller and more extremist terrorist organization LEHI. This new power constellation was further strengthened by the nomination of ex-terrorists and sympathizing veterans from the Yishuv period to key positions within the executive branches of the government. These politicians, fresh in power, were characterized by two properties: first, their ideological affinity with the Gush Emunim movement, and second, their incorporation of the methods – military, para-military and political – within their political ideas in order to counter the enemy. This composition of the government has not changed drastically since then, although in 1984 the Likud had to vacate half of the posts in favour of the national unity government. The continuity in the occupation of government ministries has explained the ongoing impact of the pro-Jewish terrorist attitude since the first assault was carried out in 1980 (under Begin's regime) and until today (the proponents of Jewish terrorism within the government have increasingly succeeded in rallying support since the outbreak of the *intifada*).

The terrorists, already very closely acquainted since their illegal settlement period with those occupying the highest executive ranks, have not had to bother convincing ideologically the already convinced. In other words, they have had no particular difficulties in mobilizing ideological sympathy. On the contrary, the propagandist efforts have been conducted mainly on the psychological level, so as to arouse feelings of shame and guilt of betrayal with the ministers, who according to the terrorists, failed to translate the commonly shared ideology into a political *fait accompli*. The terrorists have vehemently accused the government of backing down from its ideological commitments, both in its indecisive attitude towards the political organization of the Palestinian National Directive Committee, and as demonstrated in such places as Yamit and the rest of Sinai. On these grounds, so they argue, there has been left no choice for the terrorists but to complete that which the government, for various reasons, has failed to accomplish.

Plagued by contradictory and dividing emotions as to the proper political path to pursue, the government has appeared dilatory in its efforts to unravel Jewish terrorism. Even when the legal proceedings had already started, the Executive still remained reluctant to request the extradition of two suspects who fled the country to the USA. This was even more striking since the suspects did not even try to hide, nor did their supporters attempt to deny their support. Ira Rappoport (one of the escaping suspects) even gave an interview to an Israeli newspaper at that time. He voluntarily returned to Israel, and yet the authorities did not make any move to arrest him until the day (two years later) he freely handed himself over to the police. It seemed, indeed, as if the Executive made every effort possible in order to refrain from any clash whatsoever with Gush Emunim and its sympathizers. Dictated by domestic *real politik* constraints, not always compatible with the liberal democratic exigencies and bound by their declared and emotionally-felt commitment to their nationalist voters, part of the government has preferred the easy way of handling both suspects and convicted offenders.

Two among the terrorists were professional officers under the Military Governor's offices in the West Bank, others were serving as reserve officers there. A significant number of terrorists were well-known figures in West-Bank politics, occupying leading positions within the settlers' communities. As a matter of fact, the Head of the General Security Service who has, indeed, voiced his suspicions with regard to the possible existence of a Jewish terrorist organization, was prohibited for some time from pursuing the investigations and for three years a planted agent operated within the Jewish Underground. An official governmental report (the Karp Report) has pointed at the ostrich policy of the government regarding developments and events in the West Bank, thus supporting this explanation of why the terrorist assaults have remained unsolved for so long. Moreover, even when uncovering the movement, the very exposure of the terrorists and their arrests were handled in the most friendly atmosphere, marked by perfect co-operation of the terrorists with the security services.

Other factors such as family ties and professional and personal relationships between members of the Underground and persons within the Executive have played an important role in shaping the political results too. For example, out of twenty-seven terrorists and settlers, one (Moshe Sar) was known for maintaining excellent relations with the security establishment; the uncle of a second (Jehuda Cohen) was Director General of one of the governmental Ministries; a third terrorist (Josef Zruya) was son-in-law of Avner Shalev, the Director of the Department of Culture and Arts in the Ministry of Education and Culture; a fourth (Jeshua Ben-Shoshan) has been a close friend of the Minister Ariel Sharon and of the (retired) Governor of the West Bank as well as present MK Benjamin Ben-Eliezer; and another terrorist (Menachem Livni) has been said to maintain close relations with (Professor Youval Ne'eman) the ex-Minister for Science and Development and head of the Tehiya Party, as well as with the lawyer Plia Al-Beck, responsible for the land transactions (estates) within the Ministry of Justice.[29]

Briefly, this triple affinity: ideological, political and personal informal, probably explains why it took four years for the disclosure of the Jewish Underground, from its first assault in 1980, to take place. While acquaintance with the terrorists does not imply any connivance of the authorities in the crimes themselves it does, nevertheless, clearly expose the extent to which contradictory constraints have been operating: the terrorists were left untouched until the near success of the attack on the bus led to the inevitable decision to arrest them.

Overt pro-terrorist lobbying on behalf of the Executive can be traced back to the moment the Underground was publicly exposed.

Shamir, then Prime Minister, exclaimed in pathos 'do not touch my messiahs!' Those public figures close to the terrorists did not recoil from the terrorists themselves and only partially criticized their deeds. A distinction was drawn between the selective attack in 1980 on the mayors (the Heads of the National Directive Committee), and the other indiscriminate, spectacular attacks, in particular the 1984 plan to blow up the mosque on Temple Mount, which would have probably dragged the whole Islamic world into a holy war against Israel. Almost no criticism has been raised, nor has there been voiced any denunciation of the persons involved in these crimes. The sole reservations expressed referred to the deeds themselves. To be sure, a basic distinction was drawn between the deeds and the doers, so as to emphasize that the nobility of the motives overrode the atrocity of the deeds. The justification of the cause purified the terrorists, who were actually genuine 'erring sons'.

Sincere identification with the terrorists has been demonstrated on many occasions. One obvious example was given during Prime Minister Shamir's visit to the terrorists' wives. These women, who were on hunger strike in front of the Knesset (Israeli Parliament), reminded him of his underground past so much that he felt compelled to draw a parallel between the Underground and the Jewish terrorist resistance to the British mandatory rule. In a nostalgic mood he identified this kind of terrorism with his past underground experience, ignoring completely the changed political circumstances.

Moreover, identifying with the terrorists was used to stretch the analogy further back to the Yishuv's underground experience, so as to extrapolate from the policy of rehabilitation of terrorists during the early 1950s to the political environment of the 1980s. Ben-Gurion's way to merge the split camps into one nation has also required the incorporation of the ex-terrorists within the Israeli security forces as a testimony to their loyalty on the one hand, and to the beginning of a new era of trust and partnership, on the other. Evidently, the analogy made by Shamir was far too premature: the terrorists have not yet been put to trial and the task of nation-building is clearly overdue.

In practice, this attitude has been translated into a firm demand for amnesty for the terrorists, voiced by members of the executive even before the exhaustion of the legal proceedings. This lobbying theme has gained extraordinary prominence consequent to the exchange deal concluded between the Israeli government and the terrorist organization of Ahmed Jibril in 1985, whereby 1,150

Palestinian terrorists and guerrillas were set free in exchange for three Israeli soldiers held captive by Jibril's organization. Setting free the terrorists impinged on Israeli law, since many anti-terrorist trial proceedings were still pending and were illegally interrupted due to political intervention. This blackmailed exchange deal has also forced the government to pardon and set free those terrorists who were sentenced for life. Also, the terrorists were given the option to choose to stay in the Territories (under Israeli control) although it was feared they would return to terrorism. This development intensified the pressure already put on this indecisive government, plagued by guilt and feelings of shame as a result of the exchange deal.

Three lines of argument were stressed by the embittered critics of the deal: first came the moral argument, objecting to the setting free of the abominable Palestinian terrorists amongst whom were murderers of innocent citizens, including children. In the light of this, Jewish terrorists could be presented as defenders, fighting for their self-defence, not to be blamed and not guilty. Second was the political-security argument based on the presumed regression in Israel's image as a deterring opponent in its efforts against whatever kind of terrorism. The exchange deal was interpreted as encouraging terrorism to continue and, moreover, as humiliating and ridiculing all the efforts of the settlers to defend themselves against the hostile population in the midst of which they were living. The exchange deal supported their claim that the government had neglected its duty in securing them, consequently being responsible itself for driving the settlers to resort to such extreme measures as terrorism. Hence, the government should bear the blame for Jewish terrorism. The third argument attacked the legal pretence that, once such dreadful terrorists, like some among those Palestinians released, have been illegally set free, the basis of law itself has been removed. There remains no reason any more for sticking to the harsh line against indigenous Jewish terrorists. Consequently, the proponents of the Jewish Underground have urged this legal precedent not only to pardon each Jewish terrorist separately, but to grant them collective amnesty. Indeed, in the group voting on the issue, it was Prime Minister Shamir who firmly endorsed this stand.[30]

Public rhetoric and diplomatic lobbying produced practical results at the level of the police and prison authorities' handling of the terrorists. Responsible for the physical apprehension and care of the terrorists, these authorities have shown extreme laxity, deviating from regular procedures applied not only against those accused of terrorism but to common criminals as well. Unusually, the suspects were brought to their trial unchained, were allowed to move freely in court and intercourse with their families. They were released from jail for holidays and family events and enjoyed relatively free custody and imprisonment conditions: three of the terrorists were allowed to attend college regularly; two of them enjoyed the dormitory facilities of a religious college; others were permitted to teach other prisoners. At a certain point, the possibility of joining a football team outside prison was considered but failed to materialize due to strong objection. The terrorists were imprisoned in the best renovated prison quarter in the country, especially designated for young delinquents. This policy evidently reflected a positive discriminatory attitude in favour of the Underground terrorists, not only in comparison to the common and 'security prisoner', but also compared to other Jewish terrorists.

The role of the judiciary

The attitude of the judiciary towards the Jewish Underground suspects, at the beginning as well as during legal proceedings, was marked by features unprecedented in terrorist trials. For one thing, the Jewish terrorist, in contrast to the Arab-Palestinian terrorist who was also an Israeli citizen, enjoyed the privilege of being tried by a civil and not by a military court, which usually tried anti-Israeli Palestinian terrorists. The next sign of irregularity, still at the beginning of legal procedures, was the prolonged ban on the disclosure of the suspects' identity. Despite the fact that the terrorists were well-known personalities, at least within their socio-political circles and the journalist community, and that everybody in these milieux knew exactly who was arrested, the suspects were coded by numbers.

These precedents have right from the start implied the intervention of the Executive and other factors with the judicial process and procedure of the trial of the Jewish Underground. Independence of the legal authorities has been violated on several occasions. The principle of *sub judice*, prohibiting any disclosure of information or any intervention which might exert influence on the judges, which is a basic tenet of the Israeli legal system, was blatantly disregarded during this process. The demand to grant amnesty for the Jewish Underground was most strongly voiced during the exchange deal of the Israeli prisoners of war with the Arab terrorists, but surfaced every time an anti-Israeli terrorist attack was perpetrated.

The judiciary has attempted to apply a provision from the emergency rules (an inheritance from the British mandatory rule, in force since 1945) to forbid contact between suspects and their lawyers until the completion of investigations (this applied, for instance, in the case of the editors of the periodical *Derech Hanitzoz*) but has rapidly succumbed to external political pressure and renounced this intention.

Another peculiarity, typical of the characteristic events revolving around the trial of the Jewish Underground, was the multitude of plea bargains concluded between the suspects and the prosecution. At least ten out of twenty-seven succeeded in reaching agreements with the State Attorney to ease charges against them. Consequently, the most severe charge – namely membership of a terrorist organization (prohibited and coded in the Prevention of Terrorism Decree, 1948), especially formulated to counter this kind of (Jewish terrorist) offence – was dropped. Later legal developments, relating precisely to the amendment of this decree, adding the clause prohibiting meetings with the PLO (defined as a terrorist organization) have made this bargaining even more striking in its deviation from custom.

The verdicts and sentences passed by the judges have clearly deviated from the verdicts on non-Jewish terrorists, but have differed also from those decided for other Jewish terrorists who are not members of the Jewish Underground. Collective punishment, so frequently applied (by the executive and not the judiciary, however) in cases of Palestinian terrorism, was not considered at all. Today (1991), all of the twenty-seven terrorists found guilty and imprisoned have been released (some having been twice granted reduction of life sentence by the President).

To be sure, lobbying efforts have not been content with the achievements gained since the arrest of the terrorists and up to the conclusion of the trial. Amnesty, that is collective pardon, was the next goal to be pursued; if that was not achieved, then individual pardon would at least be sought. Though pardoning is the prerogative of the President and not of the judiciary, pressure from the executive on the judiciary – the Minister of Justice – encouraging him to recommend pardoning has resembled the strong lobbying taking place simultaneously within the Knesset and other public and private forums. This kind of concentrated pressure has undoubtedly influenced the President's decisions to pardon and/or ease the sentences (reducing the amount of years to be imprisoned) of seven out of twenty-seven of the terrorists. The very act of pardoning in a terrorist case and in particular the number of pardons granted as well as easing the sentences; and, on top of all, the speed with which this has occurred (less than three years after trial) have had no precedent in Israeli anti-terrorist judicial history.

Surprisingly, this law-impinging lobbying did not lead to any special repercussions in Israeli public opinion. It left no traces in the legal publications nor did it spark a reaction among the jurists. One single exception to the seeming indifference was provided by an academic symposium held on the subject of pardon and amnesty, which tried to define acceptable guidelines and criteria.[31]

Parliamentary and extra-parliamentary lobbying

Parliamentary and extra-parliamentary lobbying for Jewish terrorism has been closely related to the already prevailing mood within the public concerning the prospects for successful Jewish–Arab coexistence. The exposure of the Jewish Underground occurred at a time of sharpening and expanding extremist attitudes, hawkish and nationalist, more widely dispersed within the population than their extreme left and dovish counterparts.[32] This development in state of mind and public opinion has taken place against a background wave of sporadic, unsophisticated and poorly organized Jewish–Israeli terrorism and especially even more primitive Palestinian terrorism (1984–6). Different from previous terrorist tactics, these assaults were characterized by unsophisticated, face-to-face combat methods: an entirely unpredicted kind of terrorism, consisting mainly of lethal knife-stabbings or ambushes of loving couples. Basic, primordial feelings and attitudes towards the Arab co-citizen, towards the Palestinians ruled by Israel in the Territories and towards the Arab neighbour states and world as such, have surfaced and have been accompanied by a steady rise of anguish, suspicion and hatred. In this atmosphere of growing hostility, ever more people have started to identify with nationalist calls for an 'iron feast' policy. After all, even Israeli good will for peace with its neighbours could be considered as having almost been rejected – the 'cold peace' with Egypt was far from the eagerly expected normalization, thus adding fuel to the already burning fire. It is not surprising, then, that sympathy with Gush Emunim's erring sons has been the natural consequence.

Generally speaking, the Israeli public has been rather indecisive in its attitude towards the Underground. Yet, on special occasions, for instance the exchange deal with the PFLP occurring immediately after cruel and lethal Palestinian terrorist assaults, public opinion has tended to sympathize with the Jewish Underground, favouring pardon and amnesty. Nevertheless, public opinion was in fact selective and the attitude endorsed by it rather depended upon the nature of the crime committed: while the assaults on the leaders of the National Directive Committee were approved, reaction to the other indiscriminate assaults was more reserved. Yet, while objecting to the deeds themselves, the public has nevertheless accepted the motives and has been in sympathy with the emotions guiding the terrorists and driving them to behave violently. Interestingly, the lobby which was organized to influence public opinion nearly neglected to refer to other Jewish terrorists who were not members of the Jewish Underground, such as Ben-Shimol, Gil Fox and others. This can probably be explained by the intensive interaction between parliamentary and extra-parliamentary lobbying for the Jewish Underground, depending heavily on the political and electoral influence of Gush Emunim.

Pro-terrorist lobbying emanated from specifically defined circles within the public. Gush Emunim, various Knesset members, right-wing political parties and an impressive group of prominent rabbis formed a strong pro-terrorist lobby which endeavoured to persuade both public opinion and the judiciary to sympathize with the terrorists. The lobby has operated via official channels, including the Knesset plenum itself, as well as via unofficial ones, such as the organizations set up to support the terrorists and their families.

First in leverage comes the Gush Emunim movement and the Council of the Settlements in the Territories, representing the socio-environmental origins of the terrorists. The immediate impact of the exposure of the Underground has been a crisis within Gush Emunim, which was caught unprepared, not knowing how to react. Though most, if not all, of the assaults were at least silently approved by the movement, there has been agreement (despite important 'dissident' hard cores of identification with the terrorists and their deeds) that the deeds themselves should be denounced. In contrast, the persons involved, the terrorists, were to be treated the same as by the other lobbying circles, that is, as 'erring sons' who should be guided back to the right path deserving full rehabilitation. Commentators speculated on a split within the movement and members were worried about controversy that could disintegrate Gush Emunim. To some degree, this did indeed happen, but several years later. So, despite discrepancies, the movement has succeeded in overcoming the crisis: unified, but not free from paying the price of shifting to more radicalism, expressed in a growing inclination to engage in physically violent vigilantism.

Apart from sincere concern for its terrorist members, Gush Emunim has been seriously troubled by its image in public opinion and its popularity, especially because the movement has reached a point of stagnation.[33] After heavy discussions, the movement has settled the controversy, deciding in favour of the Jewish Underground, on the basis of the following arguments: (i) the naivety and pardonable error of the terrorists; (ii) the 'deficiencies' in the security arrangements in the Territories (the security forces allegedly being negligent in securing the safety of the settlers as well as protecting them from the daily risks. After all, it was the government that let them, and later led them to settle the Territories. Consequently, the government was required to keep its obligation and take responsibility. By not doing so, it has actually, so they argued, driven the settlers to self-defence);[34] (iii) the claim of 'a just war' and the partiality in handling the Underground terrorists and their just and relatively minor crimes in comparison to the prosecution of dreadful Palestinian terrorists; and (iv) the Underground must be understood as a passing, unique and non-recurring episode, serving as a lesson to other elements which might also have considered the use of the terrorism weapon.

Gush Emunim's efforts to mobilize more support for the terrorists were aimed at three goals: public opinion, internal group encouragement and cohesion, and the legislative authority. Through extra-parliamentary agitation, namely organizing demonstrations and processions which mainly stressed the legitimacy of the pardon or amnesty of the already convicted terrorists and required to set them free, Gush Emunim has turned to the general public for support. This activity was also directed at tightening the pressure on the government and the President (the amnesty authority) by proving to the authorities the resonance they have aroused in society. Indeed, they rightly expected to benefit as a movement from stressing the 'injustice' done to the genuinely patriotic Israelis.

Two public bodies were created to defend and assist the terrorists. The committee 'For my Brothers and Friends' (LAOR) was composed of the radical wing in Gush Emunim – Rabbi Levinger's people of Kiriyat Arba and Hebron. In contrast to Gush Emunim's declared policy, this committee did not renounce the deeds, but endorsed both the terrorists and the assaults. The committee's concern focused on public relations. In this it was blatantly impinging on the legal principle of *sub judice*, which forbids any involvement capable of influencing the judge's impartiality. In a circular, the committee declared that the formation of a sympathetic atmosphere might positively affect the sentence. The other organization, 'The Association for the Families of the Arrested' was set up for the purpose of economically sustaining the families of the terrorists. It was composed of many public figures and not of Gush Emunim members only. The wives of the terrorists appealed to the authorities by means of extra-parliamentary devices such as hunger strikes and sit-ins. A Gush Emunim 'Committee for the Arrested of the Underground' collected signatures and hung out large posters claiming an impressive number (later found to be falsified) of supporters for collective amnesty.[35]

The third battlefield of Gush Emunim was situated within the legislature. A group of parliamentarians was formed, named by the media the 'pro-terrorist lobby'. The involvement of Knesset Members (KMs) in the lobbying process has acquired various expressions. One example has been the intervention in favour of the imprisoned terrorists, directed and led by the former Minister of Science and Development and later KM, Professor Jouval Neeman, together with KM Meir Cohen-Avidav. Both have succeeded in collecting impressive financial support (in the US) to finance the terrorists' trial and hire the best advocates. KMs like Geula Cohen and Dov Shilansky exhibited their support for the terrorists through spectacular 'propagandist' gestures such as visits to jail and extensive media coverage. Other KMs concentrated on rhetoric activity and public relations, organizing meetings, interviews and visits in the settlements of the terrorists and their families. They have incessantly handed in appeals to the President, Mr Haim Herzog, requesting amnesty for the terrorists in this way also increasing their electoral prospects. Apparently, among the explanations for the personnel changes within the religious MAFDAL party has been the degree of support expressed for the terrorists. This party, as others from the right wing, lent its offices and supplied facilities to the pro-terrorist lobbying activists. Indeed, pro-Jewish terrorism attitudes have become an issue serving electoral purposes the same way that nurturing anti-Palestinian terrorism positions has done since the exposure of Jewish terrorism. The Tehiya Party even considered introducing one of the already released ex-terrorists as 'honorary candidate' on its election list (1988).

All the terrorist supporters within the Knesset united in a motion calling for the enactment of a 'General Amnesty Law' especially tailored to collectively pardon the Jewish Underground terrorists only, so as to bypass the regular procedure of individual pardon. The motion failed, although it was vehemently endorsed by Prime Minister Shamir and there was widespread support in favour of the bill. Lobbying efforts targeting ministers, in particular, the Minister of Justice and the Prime Minister, have pressured them to persuade the President to pardon the terrorists as well as urging them to exert influence on the prison authorities to grant special and privileged treatment to the Underground prisoners.

Expanding lobbying efforts to non-political religious fora was a natural next step to follow. Close to the opening of the trial sixty rabbis met publicly to declare their refusal to recognize the terrorists as criminal offenders. They rebuffed the charges and found the requirement for an expression of the terrorist's regret about the assaults committed by them as redundant. Only later, when chances for a collective amnesty and pardon seemed weakened, did the rabbis recommend such a public declaration of regret from the terrorists to be issued. In line with KM's involvement, the High Sephardic Rabbi has borne character witness for one of the terrorists.

Compared to the volume and multitude of the pro-terrorist lobby's voice, those circles opposed to any partiality in the treatment of the terrorists and in the attitude towards terrorism at large, have been rather marginal. Due to their extraordinarily well organized system as well as to their talent in recruiting the assistance of already existing powerful institutions, the lobbyists have gained far more impact on public opinion and on the authorities, than have the silent majority.

Finally, there has also been a core of supporters for Jewish-Israeli terrorism among particular circles of US Jewry. There is no doubt that Jewish immigrants to Israel did actually engage in terrorism, though specifically in the TNT organization, the members of which were among the adherents of the extreme nationalist movement (later the party), Kach. Four of these terrorists had already met during their political activity in the USA, in the League for Jewish Defense established by ex-KM Rabbi Meir Kahane. This organization has been active especially in California and New York, and some of its members have been arrested, tried and imprisoned by US authorities. It has also served, along with its splinter Jewish Terrorist organization, the United Militant Jewish Front which was involved in terrorism against Arab and Soviet targets in the USA (a bomb planted in 1985 in the offices of the American-Arab Anti-Discrimination Committee caused the death of the regional director and the wounding of eight persons) as a pool for Israeli terrorists, recruited from among its members immigrating to Israel. Indeed, Ira Rappoport, member of the Jewish Underground, is an example.[36] Another point worth mentioning is that conservative circles within American Jewry, which sustain the Gush Emunim Movement, have also engaged in financially supporting the Underground terrorists (after their exposure).

CONCLUSION

A comparison between pro-Palestinian terrorism efforts and pro-Jewish terrorism lobbying reveals clearly that these phenomena belong to two different environments. In other words, despite the common denominator of supporting extremely violent political be-haviour (terrorism), there prevails a basic asymmetry, indeed contradiction, between both lobbies. Moreover, both lobbies mutu-ally complete each other since, though separately, they exhaust all the possibilities available for the support of terrorism. This is the case not only of nearly tolerating terrorism, but of support as well.

A comparative study of Jewish terrorist activities in Palestine and later, in Israel, has revealed that the sources of support for the terrorists have basically remained the same.[37] The main novelty has been the expansion of the ideological and political basis to include an ever-growing portion within the Jewish-Israeli public. In other words, universal (liberal democratic) human values have stepped back in favour of nationalist-ideological ones. A normative gnawing has taken place, empirically manifested in public life and expressed by the retreat from an absolute rejection of terrorism to a comparative attitude distinguishing between just and unjust terrorism. Perhaps this attitude was latent, yet suppressed and contained all the time during which Israel experienced Palestinian terrorism, and has now found the opportunity to surface and expose itself (since Israeli society has enjoyed a long period devoid of Jewish terrorism). Once such terrorism was launched, the whole and authentic public attitude towards the enemy and terrorism could come to light. Specific Israeli circumstances – the general shift to the right, the disputed Lebanon War, the election of a racist party into the Knesset (1984), inflation, laxity and loss of control and decisiveness on behalf of the executive, judicial and legislative authorities – all together enabled an 'understanding' for indigenous terrorism, directed against the enemy, as part of a search for drastic and decisive solutions in a time of uncertainty and distress. Consequently, a pro-terrorist lobby was able to find fertile ground to act legitimately and even cover all spheres of Israeli public life.

Pro-Palestinian terrorism supporters have basically remained the same, while having succeeded in expanding the circles of sympathizers to the international scene. This expansion has not originated in a Palestinian-oriented awareness only, but profited from the all-encompassing trend to identify and sustain any movement of national liberation. It has benefited from the change effected in human morality and ethics, turning people's right to self-determination to compete with the value of human life and liberty. It has thus often contradicted and clashed with the rejection of violence as a means to settle disputes, failing to differentiate between the crime itself, the motivation and the equal rights of the offender as a human being.

Operating in more than one legal system and motivated by rival political aspirations, the pro-Palestinian terrorist lobby has found mainly external channels of expression, while the pro-Jewish terrorism supporters have benefited from the support of those within the domestic field only. This separation has important implications concerning the Jewish–Palestinian conflict. They are, however, beyond the scope of this study.

NOTES

1   Gal-Or, Noemi, 'The Israeli Defence Forces and Unconventional Warfare: The Palestinian Factor and Israeli National Security Doctrine', *The Journal of Terrorism and Political Violence*, Summer 1990, p. 28.
2   Our study is limited to the period ending December 1988, when patterns of socio-political behaviour drastically changed. Terrorism as part of the *Intifada* (popular Palestinian uprising in the Territories) has acquired dimensions different from those previously prevailing and so have the efforts to support the violent protestors.
3   Elam, Yigal, *The Zionist Way to Power*, Tel Aviv, Zmora, Bitan, Modan Publishers, 1979, pp. 29–177.
4   Gal-Or, Noemi, *The Jewish Underground: Our Terrorism*, Tel Aviv, Hakibbutz Hameuchad, Kav Adom Series, 1990.

5   *Tzomet Hasharon,* 26 February 1988, pp. 36–7, 41; Langer, Felicia, *With My Own Eyes,* Israel, Machberet Publishers, 1974.
6   *Haaretz,* 17 February 1987, p. 4; 20 February 1987, p. 2b.
7   Gal-Or, Noemi, 'Countering Terrorism in Israel', *Meeting the Challenge of International Terrorism: Comparative Democratic Responses,* Fredericton, Centre for Conflict Studies, New Brunswick University, forthcoming.
8   *Haaretz,* 26 April 1988, p. 5; 2 May 1988, p. 2; 3 May 1988, pp. 1, 7; 6 May 1988, p. 8b.
9   Op cit., 27 November 1987, p. 3b. Pinchas Inbari underscores the role of Quakers' activity among the Palestinian population, dating back to 1896. From a purely philanthropic engagement this has changed to also serve American political interests in the Middle East. This transformation took place especially in 1974 under the guise of the 'Centre for Information and Legal Assistance' specializing in legal assistance to terrorists, something absolutely contrary to Quakers' pacifist vocation. See Pinchas Inbari, *Triangle on the Jordan,* Tel Aviv: Sifriat Maariv, 1982.
10 *Haaretz,* 9 September 1986, p. 3; 12 September 1986, p. 3b; 16 September 1986, p. 11; *Koteret Rashit,* 3 September 1986, p. 7.
11 *Haaretz,* 14 October 1987, p. 11.
12 *Haaretz,* 8 July 1985, p. 7.
13 The Sabena aircraft hijacking, 8 May 1972; the Savoy Hotel assault, 5 March 1975; the Coastal Highway Bus attack, March 1978, and many other terrorist attempts.
14 Gal-Or, Noemi 'Suppressing Terrorism: Problems of European – Israeli Cooperation', in *Europe and Israel: Troubled Neighbours,* Ilan Greilsammer and Joseph H.H. Weiler (eds), Berlin, Walter de Gruyter, 1988, pp. 329–37
15 *Davar,* 27 October 1986, p. 3; *Haaretz,* 30 September 1986, p. 9; March 1987, p. 5; 20 April 1988, p. 6.
16 *Al Hamishmar,* 26 September 1986, p. 2; *Haaretz,* 30 September 1986, p. 9; 1 December 1987, p. 4; 6 April 1988, p. 5; 6 May 1988, pp. 1a, 9a.
17 *Haaretz,* 22 May 1985, p. 7; 23 May 1985, p. 3; 9 June 1985, p. 9.
18 Kanovsky, Eliyahu, 'The Rise and Fall of the Arab Oil Power', *Middle East Review,* Vol. 18 (1), 1985, pp. 6–8
19 Gal-Or, 'Countering Terrorism'.
20 We content ourselves by mentioning the fact without supplying further evidence since the literature relevant to this issue is well known and extensive.
21 Al-Peleg, Zvi, '"Independent Palestine" in the Entanglement of Inter-Arab Hostility 1946–49', *Maarachot* 294–5, July 1984, pp. 52– 66.
22 Israeli reprisal tactics launched in retaliation to terrorist assaults have been frequently interpreted as aggressive intervention. Of course, the PLO Geneva Declaration, 15 December 1988, refers also to a change in the organization's attitude towards terrorism (also Palestinian) and counter-terrorism efforts.
23 See above, n. 14; Gal-Or, Noemi, 'The Pendulum of Arab International Transportation Terrorism', in *The 1986 Annual on Terrorism,* ed. Yonah

Alexander, Dordrecht: Martinus Nijhoff, 1987, pp.177– 89.

24   *Bamachane*, special issue on 'Terrorism', No. 42, 22 July 1987, p. 20.

25   *Haaretz*, 26 October 1984, p. 15.

26   Rabbis Benjamin and Jacob Petersil (Eds), *Against Terrorism: Essays, Articles, Memoranda, Discourses*, Jerusalem, August 1939; Niv, David, *Essays, Notes, Conversations*, Jerusalem: Brit Hayalei Haezel Beserushalayim, 1987.

27   Gal-Or, *The 'Jewish Underground'*, passim.

28   Aronoff, Myron J. 'Gush Emunim: The Institutionalization of a Charismatic, Messianic Religious-political Revitalization Movement in Israel', in *Religion and Politics*, ed. Arnoff, *Political Anthropology*. Vol. 3, New Brunswick: Transaction Books, 1984; Raanan, Zvi, *Gush Emunim*. Tel Aviv: Sifriat Hapoalim, 1980; Oz, Amos, *A Journey in Israel. Autumn 1982*, Tel Aviv: Am Oved, 1984.

29   Gal-Or, *Jewish Underground*.

30   *Haaretz*, 21 May 1985, p. 1; 24 May 1985, p. 15; 9 July 1987, pp. 1, 6.

31   'Discourse on the Subject of Pardon', *Mishpatim* Vol. 15 (6), 1985, pp. 9–20.

32   In 1984 a racist party succeeded for the first time in Israeli history to get elected. Kach was later banned by a Supreme Court decision in late 1988.

33   Either because of its rapid success on the operational level of the settlement policy or the contrary, the changing character of the settlers – from nationalist-ideologists to economically profit-oriented pragmatists. To this must be added the agreement between both parties forming the then national unity government concerning the halt in the establishment of new settlements.

34   Self-protection has a double meaning: (i) physical, personal and immediate necessity, and (ii) a national, ideological imperative to prevent any crystallization whatsoever of Palestinian national organization which might endanger Israeli hegemony in the Territories. For more see, Gal-Or, *The 'Jewish Underground'* about the role of the security forces and the military government and the vacuum created to be abused by the settlers.

35   *Haaretz*, 19 June 1985, p. 3; *Haiir*, 12 June 1987, p. 19. Choice of terrorism as method to solve the political problem of Israel, perceived in terms of an existential threat, was endorsed by 40 per cent of Jewish youth and justified on religious grounds by religious youngsters. *Haaretz*, 12 June 1987, p. 3a; 10 April 1985, p. 3.

36   *Mussaf Haaretz*, 9 May 1986, pp. 12–15; *Haaretz*, 28 August 1986, p. 7

37   Gal-Or, *Jewish Underground*.

Chapter 4

The CCC phenomenon in Belgium: unbacked terrorism

Simon Petermann

Since the arrest of the recognized leader of the CCC and some confederates in December 1985, no further acts of violence have been perpetrated in Belgium. It is undoubtedly too early to conclude that henceforth, Belgium will be spared from terrorism. The terrorist phenomenon is – alas – an ecliptical one, unpredictable, and can resurge for reasons unknown which sometimes are more related to developments on the international scene than the national context.[1]

When, on 2 October 1984, a first attack struck the company LITTON Business Belgium, a multinational specializing in telecommunications, Belgium was plunged into consternation. The Belgians in fact, discovered to their amazement that their country was no longer sheltered from the wave of terrorism which had swept nearly all of Europe. They were amazed because Belgium had until then been rather a peaceful country where political, social or community violence did not find a favourable breeding ground. And yet, in the space of a fortnight, there were five bomb attacks against multinationals working more or less closely with the NATO military programme and against the Parti Réformateur Libéral (PRL) (Liberal Reform Party) in Brussels and the Christelijke Volkspartji (CVP) (Christian People's Party) in Ghent, two of the coalition government parties. Responsibility for this first series of attacks was claimed by the mysterious 'Cellules Communistes Combattantes' (CCC) (Fighting Communist Cells) of which no one had ever heard. The CCC distributed communiqués on each occasion, sometimes very lengthy ones, written in language intelligible only to the initiated, explaining their aims, with supporting photos of their targets.[2]

It was thus, that between 2 October 1984 and 16 December 1985 the CCC claimed responsibility for twenty-one bomb attacks in the framework of the 'anti-imperialist campaigns', also known as the 'Karl Marx' or 'Pierre Akkerman' campaign, the latter after a Belgian communist volunteer in the international brigades in Spain, killed in combat in January 1937.[3]

On each occasion the CCC showed unusual audacity. All the attacks committed by them were meant to be demonstrative. Apart from the attack on 1 May 1985 which killed two firemen, they endeavoured to avoid injury by using leaflets, taped messages or a telephone call a few minutes prior to the explosion, to warn the people in the vicinity of the site where the attack was to take place.

In the eyes of the investigators, these communiqués placed the CCC from the outset in the sphere of influence of terrorism of Marxist-Leninist or left-wing inspiration. They identified their enemy as being primarily 'Imperialism' with NATO as its very incarnation. They were also against the Belgian state and its government ('NATO's vassal'), who were 'in the pay of the United States and her aggressive policy'. Their No. 1 communiqué was clear, a veritable declaration of war on 'middle-class' society, and a call on the workers to insurrection: 'Let's organise ourselves and hit without respite. Forward towards the construction of a fighting and proletarian organisation which will undertake the communist revolution. All power to the workers.' These calls to insurrection alternated, according to the targets aimed at, with calls for civil disobedience and reflections on social injustices or the high cost of electricity. Crammed with quotations from the Communist Party Manifesto, Engels and Lenin and with references to 'Comrade Stalin', the communiqués, which were often repetitive, also referred to actions taken during the previous ten years by the RAF (Red Army Faction) or the BR (Red Brigade). To the CCC, the German, Italian, Basque and Irish terrorists were exemplary figures in the revolutionary campaign.

Justification for armed struggle and urban guerrilla warfare was, in fact, directly inspired by the RAF and BR campaigns. In both, the distinction was made between the military combat phase and the political phase. In the first, it was a question of organizing armed struggle in the form of urban guerrilla warfare directed against the state; in the second, this guerrilla warfare took on the dimensions of a political plan aimed at eradicating the last remains of middle-class society and its allies in the worker movement('revisionists' in the Maoist jargon of the 1960s). The pacifists who at the time demonstrated against the deployment of euromissiles came in for no better treatment by the CCC.[4]

According to CCC statements, this identification with other terrorist groups did not go beyond an ideological community. Furthermore, they stressed their specifically national character, while recognizing that in the interests of the revolution it was crucial that certain links be established with other European organizations, particularly on questions of logistics.[5]

What was striking in the case of the CCC was the contrast between the archaism of their ideology and the 'modernism' of their campaign methods. In a long communiqué sent to the press in May 1985, they did not hesitate to describe at length their 'work methods': collection of documents; review of targets; photographs of target sites; 'proletarian expropriations' carried out in banks in order to obtain the necessary financial means . . . It should be added that they appeared in some sense more 'modern' than their European counterparts in the use made of the media (specifically the written press, for obvious reasons of anonymity). As a matter of fact, the press hastened to reproduce long extracts from the communiqués, thus ensuring the CCC had wide publicity. The audacity of their methods, the choice of symbolic targets (multinationals, NATO, the 'employers', the 'middle-class' parties), the precautions taken to avoid injury, explain to a large extent the strange fascination that the CCC exerted on several journalists not accustomed to dealing with local terrorism.[6]

One could say that popular perception of the CCC took the form of three successive figures which constituted stereotype images: the honourable outlaw, the professional and the manipulated.

The first attacks hit multinational companies (without injury) and provoked no indignation among the people: rather, a concerned curiosity at these strange Robin Hoods playing cat and mouse with the forces of order. In fact, it was this image of the noble outlaw, the righter of wrongs, he who defended the 'small' against the 'big', which prevailed in the first instance. However, these images, which were taken up by the media, were rapidly swept away as a result of the repetitive nature of the attacks, to be replaced by the image of the professional terrorist.

The image of the professional gained credence because the CCC seemed particularly well informed about their targets, their actions were carefully planned and they had a large arsenal at their disposal. The idea that the CCC formed the Belgian branch of a sort of Terrorist International, with its own financial resources, multiple networks, and whose central figures were Abu Nidal, Carlos or J.M. Rouillan, the leader of Action Directe in France, thus gained ground. This idea was to be reinforced when the police discovered that Action Directe leaflets had been printed in Belgium, that some of its members were in hiding there, that explosives used in a certain number of attacks were stolen from a quarry in Ecaussines in June 1984, and that weapons were passed on and exchanged from one organization to another.

This hypothesis of a 'Belgian branch' was obviously taken into consideration by the investigators, but no sustaining evidence came to light during the enquiry. However, what was certain was that the principal figure in the CCC, Pierre Carette, arrested in December 1985, had links with Action Directe. Born in 1952, the son of a Belgian Security Service agent a former student of the Brussels Fine Arts Academy, artisan-printer, and leader of a 'Defence Committee for Political Prisoners in the FRG', Carette was a left-winger whose political intinerary resembled that of several former 'sixty-eighters'.[7] However, unlike others, he did not change tune. He felt at home in the nebula of the extreme left. Moreover, he was an action fanatic, totally devoted to armed struggle. His natural bent led him very quickly to make contact with the Action Directe terrorists in France (particularly Nathalie Ménigon) for whom he covertly printed leaflets and also provided hide-outs. He also circulated a magazine provocatively entitled *Subversion*, whose principal characteristic was the vindication of 'anti-imperialist struggles' in the Third World.[8] Carette, however, was nothing like the ideal international terrorist stereotype; he frequented training camps in neither the Lebanon nor Libya, though he has had links with the FARL (Lebanese Armed Revolutionary Faction).[9] If he is in police files, it is as a left-wing activist and not as a dangerous terrorist.[10]

However that may be, the idea that the CCC constituted an organization linked to obscure foreign forces was to mark public opinion. In 1985, as a climate of insecurity installed itself in Belgium, following a series of brutal and bloody hold-ups (the 'mad killers' of walloon Brabant) which were to be added to the CCC attacks, the idea that the CCC was the driving force and instrument of a Machiavellian conspiracy of totally different political inspiration was repeatedly penned by certain journalists in the press, without an ounce of proof being offered. Over and above the amalgam between gangsters and terrorists, it was the explanation in terms of manipulation which was to be put forward the most often. In place of the image of the professional terrorist, that of the 'great conspiracy' was substituted, where, from the extreme right to the extreme left, from neo-Nazis to ex-Maoists, from the KGB to the CIA who were looking to 'counter the pacifist movement which is becoming too powerful in Europe', a whole world of double agents was to emerge who were manipulating each other or being manipulated.

For some, the means at the disposal of gangster killers and terrorists to lead such 'efficient' campaigns were an indication of a 'foreign' presence which could equally well be Moscow, Tripoli or Washington; Belgium, hitherto spared the terrorist phenomenon, had become the focal point and was overtaken by events. For others, the high level of organization of the terrorist-gangsters, their audacity, the impunity which they seemed to have at their disposal, directed the search towards 'second zone politicians, university professors, lawyers' who would be the veritable masterminds of a destabilization strategy.[11]

These amalgams and phantasmagoric interpretations originated from the Belgian state's powerlessness to exercise its constitutional functions, at least in the early days, and from the conservatism of an initially indifferent (or, worse, amused) public opinion, subsequently alarmed by the rise of insecurity. To that was added the fact that the communist and left-wing organizations, embarrassed by the ideological proximity of the CCC, looked consciously or subconsciously to directing the attention of the public, the authorities and especially the media, towards right-wing terrorism.

Thus, when the Belgian government, after setting up a joint services anti-terrorist staff, on 1984 October 19 ordered a huge search operation known as 'Mammoth' directed against extreme left-wing organizations or those presumed to be such, the Parti du Travail de Belgique (Work Party of Belgium), the 22nd March Committee, the Europe–Latin America Committee, the weekly *Pour* and personalities with left-wing tendencies (Olivier Deleuze, Ecology MP; Roger Noël, known as Babar, radio announcer; Yves de Wasseige, the son of a socialist senator) the protests were lively.

These protests came essentially from left-wing personalities who denounced the political, anti-democratic, even illegal nature of the operation. A petition protesting against the searches was circulated in university circles. It is true that only those organizations in the left-wing sphere of influence were visited and that extreme-right circles were spared. The Minister of Justice, Jean Gol, replied that all the clues pointed to 'circles close to the distorted extreme-left, that is to say the extreme-left-wing movements who have become violent.'[12]

This declaration led to a statement by the communist party in the following terms: 'the pseudo-marxist jargon of the CCC has fooled no-one; it is known that the political terrorism of small groups is absolutely alien to Marxist tradition.'[13] It is true that no member of the communist party was at any moment of the enquiry suspected of belonging to the CCC. Generally speaking, the extreme left-wing circles, although targeted by the investigators, carefully avoided defending the CCC. Despite ideological proximity with the CCC – both share the same simplistic vision of the world as inherited in May 1968 and of its disillusions – the Belgian left-wingers hid behind careful reserve.

The dissenting Belgian left-wing movements, though strongly influenced by their foreign counterparts, notably the French, were not merely an extension of them. May 1968 did not have the same repercussions in Belgium as in France. In Belgium, left-wing movements found support mainly in universities and schools. In general, the labour movement remained deaf to calls for revolution. The few outbursts provoked by left-wing elements found no echoes in a country where trade unions are traditionally strong and closely linked to political parties, where the level of membership of trade unions is among the highest in the world, and where linguistic divisions largely dominate political life. It is a fact that trade unions, and in particular those exposed to the actions of extremists in the event of spontaneous strikes, reacted vigorously against agitation from student quarters.

Left-wing movements of all types (anarchists, Maoists, Trotskyists, etc.) have been most evident in the organization (often with considerable success) of campaigns in support of Third World countries, of anti-militarist demonstrations, and of collective action in defence of the rights of immigrant workers, of victims of racism and xenophobia, and in a general sense of those rejected by society. Contrary to their counterparts in France, Germany and Italy, the left in Belgium has rarely had recourse to violence in furthering their aims. If the left has espoused the cause of the Third World, and in particular the struggle of the Palestinians, recourse to terrorism has never been seen as a means of achieving its ends. The majority take the view that acts of violence are provocative and ultimately work to the advantage of the right and the extreme right, when the organizations which espouse violence are not already indirectly infiltrated by these.

This resulted in a rather ambivalent attitude towards the CCC. In fact the left-wingers, or some of them, considered that the CCC was made up of 'comrades' mistaken in their tactics and strategy, but whose motivations or frustrations were understandable. More often, the CCC phenomenon was denounced as organized extreme-right manipulation. Only a few dozen anarchists demonstrated their support of the CCC publicly on the occasion of a demonstration in Brussels in October 1985, or more anonymously by means of graffiti on the walls of the capital.

We have seen how the theory according to which the CCC is only an emanation of the extreme right was taken up by certain journalists. This was especially true following a wave of attacks directed against the Bierset military base and the NATO pipeline network in Wallonia (December 1984).

The minute detail that went into the preparation of these attacks resurrected in the press the idea of an extreme-right conspiracy (the neo-Nazi Westland New Post clique, a small neo-Nazi organization, some members of which were then on trial for common criminal acts, was often to be quoted) linked to certain activist circles in the army who supposedly delivered the necessary plans to enable such an attack to happen. In reality, no evidence was ever produced to support this view, which rests on political fiction in a country where the extreme right is marginal, and which, on top of this, is divided by linguistic differences. Links between the extreme right and gendarmes or military personnel, if they existed at all, were too slight to destabilize Belgium. The instigation of a 'strategy of tension' as in Italy, sometimes mentioned in the press, assumes not only the existence of a secret service controlling and guiding developments with the objective of strengthening the position of the establishment or serving the interests of foreign powers, but also a serious crisis of government, which was very evidently not the case at the time. The PCB (Belgian Communist Party) went one better at the time, proclaiming 'that the CCC attacks are of a precise nature and orientation: they objectively support those who claim to be in favour of the basing of nuclear missiles in Florennes' (communiqué of 11 December 1984). Nevertheless the judiciary directed enquiries towards the ultra-left. The fact that the enquiries made but little progress for some considerable time can be explained by the unusual nature of the events, their extent, and above all by a lack of co-ordination between the various services handling a dossier which quickly swelled with an accumulation of documents.

The arrest of four members of the CCC in mid-December 1985 put an end to the 'loss of reason' which characterized the press commentaries at the height of the second CCC 'campaign'. To be sure, the misuse of the media by the CCC also contributed to create this impression. In perpetrating their terrorist attacks at the same time as murders were being committed by the gang known as the 'Mad Killers', the CCC added to the confusion between terrorists and gangsters made by the press and public opinion, without at any time condemning the crimes, or distancing themselves from the gangsters. This serious error was a consequence of a loss of purpose and misjudgment which allowed the press to look for an explanation for the phenomenon of terrorism on an international level, although the CCC had sought to focus their actions within the context of Belgian society.

Yet, until that arrest, the CCC remained small and seemed even to have some emulators. In fact, several attacks of an unsophisticated nature against the Secretariat of the North Atlantic Assembly, against buildings belonging to the AEG Telefunken company and against offices of the Bayer Belgium company, were claimed to be the work of a mysterious 'FRAP' (Revolutionary Front for Proletarian Action). Although the CCC hastened to dissociate themselves from the FRAP, their targets were identical. The arrest of a few suspects in June 1985, one of which José Alvarez-Costales, had links with the Spanish FRAP, enabled investigators to uncover connections between the FRAP and the CCC.

Public opinion was only really outraged when two firemen lost their lives in the attack perpetrated by the CCC on 1 May 1985 against the headquarters of the Belgian employers' organization in Brussels. The date was symbolic. Hitting out on the day, the CCC wanted to celebrate Labour Day in their own way. They only succeeded in inciting unanimous public opinion against themselves.

The change in public opinion was more complex than a simple switch from surprise to fear. As a matter of fact, from evident indifference at the outset, public opinion became seriously concerned with the threat of terrorism and became increasingly insistent in its demands that the state exercise its authority to curb terrorism. Yet, the forces of law and order appeared weak and indecisive, despite the considerable resources at their disposal. It should be borne in mind that at more than 30,000, Belgium's Police Force is well above the average size for European countries (twice that of the Netherlands, and equal to that of Canada). What concerned public opinion most was the number of violent crimes which remained unsolved. As a result, questions on the appearance of terrorism in Belgium were no longer discussed in a European or international context as had been the initial approach of the press, but were placed in the national context where the problem of the repression of terrorism was to become a central issue.

Here, too, lessons drawn from the past and from foreign experience were introduced into the debate. It was generally agreed that it was essential to avoid falling into a cycle of provocation–repression, as had happened in Italy and Germany, to the detriment of the liberal legal structure which has been a characteristic of the Belgian constitution since 1830. But it was also accepted that the state should fully assume its responsibility for the maintenance of law and order. When units of armed para-commandos reinforced patrols of gendarmes in the larger Belgian cities, public opinion felt reassured.

The climate of insecurity which reigned at the time and which has already been referred to above, brought about wide consensus between government and public opinion for the first time since the CCC first appeared. But this consensus was expressed in terms of both the firmness and the limits which should apply to anti-terrorist activities: fundamental liberties should not be put into question, but the aims of terrorism must be thwarted through the promulgation by the state of emergency laws – insistence had to be on a better co-ordination of the forces of order. As a Belgian sociologist has written: 'Over and above fear and insecurity, it is the term of moderated conservatism which can best describe the state of public opinion on the eve of the arrest of four members of the Cells.'[14]

In conclusion, the CCC phenomenon represents an 'unbacked terrorism', that is to say a terrorism which has no bearing on reality, produced by a small political group, cut off from any social movement, looking inwards at its ideological world. Its ability to survive for more than a year was due to the fact that it came up against forces of order ill-prepared for the fight against national terrorism and public indifference. When the Belgian government demonstrated its authority, this time backed by public opinion, the CCC tried to find an international escape route by strengthening ties with Action Directe or the West German RAF. But these ties, at the time of Pierre Carette's arrest, were still too tenuous for them to have been able to do anything to save the terrorist organization. In the end, the CCC terrorists did not find the support in Belgium that they had reckoned on. By their sectarianism and their ideological dogmatism, they alienated themselves from those left-wingers whose psychic make-up could lead them to embark on the road of terrorism. The future alone will tell us whether the CCC phenomenon was just an epiphenomenon linked to the decline of the extreme left, or whether it was the forerunner to a serious crisis in Belgian society.

NOTES

1   Indeed, acts of terrorism committed in Belgium before 1984 can be directly associated with aspects of the Israeli–Palestinian conflict: attacks on the Jewish communities of Antwerp and Brussels, murder of the representative of the PLO in Brussels, etc. These acts of terrorism did not fail to arouse the indignation of Belgian public opinion, but they remained detached from events of national concern, even though the victims were Belgian Jews.

2   A relevant detail: the date of the attack was always indicated by the use of a date stamp applied in a space left blank for that purpose.

3   Documents seized at their hide-outs after the arrest of members of the CCC show that many acts of violence were being planned, including attacks on individuals (the financier Albert Frère, the ex-minister Mark Eyskens and Freddy Vreven and others).

4   A leader of the pacifist movement, Pierre Galand, was even the target of an attack with a Molotov cocktail.

5   It should be stressed that the CCC are an offspring of the last convulsions of left-wing activists operating on European scale and are not to be seen as a feature of an ascendant movement. This also explains the tenuous nature of links with counterparts in other countries. Subsequent investigations revealed, however, that Belgian, French and German terrorists shared to a large extent their support bases and their logistical backup such as the supply of arms, explosives and false identity documents. During the 1980s, Belgium became to some extent a safe-haven for a number of Italian, French and German terrorists, who survived only because this international refuge was available. A traditional channel in the arms trade, it was also in Belgium that pamphlets were printed, which served to feed internal debates. Moreover, it was a printer, Pierre Carette, who formed the CCC in 1984.

6   Indeed, in the early stages, it was due to the support of the media that the CCC achieved their objectives of transmitting ideological messages to the general public.

7   The extreme-left's lawyer, Michel Graindorge, compared Pierre Carette to Netcheiev, the Russian terrorist.

8   This magazine was launched by Frédérich Oriach, a kind of apostle of political violence in France, who holds strong anti-Zionist views. He

was later found guilty and condemned for association with criminals (the FARL) following a wave of violence in France during the summer of 1984 against the Goldenberg restaurant and two Israeli companies, Ganco and the Leumi Bank.

9   It seems that Carette printed an FARL leaflet claiming responsibility for the assassination on 22 April 1982 of the Israeli diplomat, Yacob Barsimantov.

10   During his trial, Carette – and his associates – remained faithful to their beliefs. He denounced 'bourgeois justice' and claimed the status of a political prisoner.

11   Offergeld, J. and Souris C., *Euroterrorisme: la Belgique étranglée*, Montigny-le-Tilleul: Scaillet, 1985, p. 299.

12   *Le Soir*, 22 October 1984.

13   *Ibid.*

14   Francq, B. 'Les Cellules communistes combattantes: les deux figures d'une inversion', *Sociologie du Travail*, 4, 1986, p. 467.

Chapter 5

Terrorism supporters in the west: the Italian case

Francesco Sidoti

PECULIARITIES OF ITALIAN TERRORISM

In Italy the word 'terrorism' has been used with reference to actions characterized by:

1 use of illegal violence for political purposes
2 creation of intimidation, fear, apprehension
3 random murder of innocent people
4 targets chosen for symbolic reasons.

All of these characteristics are not found in every terrorist operation. For instance, not every act of Italian terrorism was perpetrated against random people; often the targets were cautiously selected, and sometimes the act created no special fear in the population. Moreover, there have been many kinds of terrorism: some linked to historical ethnic contrasts like those existing in the South Tyrol border area, others connected with conflicts in the Middle East, and many originated from specific Italian cleavages like the opposition between right- and left-wing groups. The Italian terroristic events are confused with the darkest events of recent Italian political life, from mafia crimes to covert operations ruled by local and foreign secret services. The exceptional intensity of the terrorist struggle, the great number of victims, the innuendoes about a low-level warfare ruled by secret services are the most important peculiarities of Italian terrorism compared with those of other industrial democracies.

A leading American scholar of Italian politics has written in a book much appreciated by many researchers: 'Even today, many intellectuals will insist that much of the terrorism in the country is an emanation of the multinationals, often aided by intelligence services like the CIA. Books on the Moro case continue to appear, full of insinuations . . .'[1] In his ponderous study of terrorism, M. Wieviorka distinguishes two specific phenomena of the Italian society: the survival of a fascist or neofascist political tendency which is tolerated within institutions like the Catholic Church or the Christian Democratic Party and a more subterranean right-wing tendency, sustained by people who have very important positions within the secret services and the army. In Wieviorka's opinion, it's 'quite probable' that these two tendencies are connected, and it is possible to see 'the mark of foreign interventions and especially that of the CIA'.[2]

On the basis of completely different hypotheses, the secret services of other countries, belonging to opposite spheres of influence, have been indicated as responsible for involvement in Italian terrorism. Strong suspicion has fallen especially on the Soviet Union and other eastern European states like Bulgaria (particularly with reference to the shooting of Pope John Paul II in Rome) and Czechoslovakia (particularly with reference to the training of the first Italian terrorists). Soviets, moreover, have been accused several times and with full particulars of carrying on a misleading campaign about American intentions, in order to convince westerners that the United States is primarily to blame for international terrorism.[3]

Foreign secret services have been *suspected* many times and from different points of view; the Italian secret services have been openly *accused* of being involved for a long time in an organized conspiracy which has directed terrorist events (above all the most bloody ones). Many observers, such as judges or journalists, have believed in suspicions and allegations of various kinds. In 1988, a parliamentary committee was instituted 'to evaluate the results of the struggle against terrorism and to examine the causes which have prevented the identification of the culprits of the massacres'. The experience of previous parliamentary investigations into the mafia, the Sindona case and the pseudo-Masonic lodge P2 are not encouraging.[4] The anti-mafia committee was known as 'the dangerous powder magazine which never explodes' and was even declared 'very disreputable' in a high-court decision. Once, a freshly elected member of the anti-mafia committee made his entrance to the committee meeting asserting: 'I am here to defend my honour and that of my friends'. At that time, this representative was thrown out of the committee of inquiry due to those assertions; and today, at least in the initial statements, if there is some person who is in the terrorism committee to defend the lost honour of sordid friends, he will be more cautious and more subtle (but not less biased) in his arguments.

Frequently, majority and minority reports of these previous committees were antagonistic both on important problems and less relevant ones. Incidental unanimity was evaluated as exceptional, and consequently 'suspicious' by many observers. Other observers have stressed that very often the itinerary of investigation seemed to be chosen before the beginning of the inquiry, and that convenient facts were selected to confirm the previously chosen hypothesis; certainly, some conclusions have been formed solely on the basis of membership: too often politicians (and sometimes scholars too) have been manipulated into endorsing the policy of the lobby that recruits them. It is difficult to oppose the opinion of the employer and it is easy to find confirmation for almost any type of hypothesis, even of the wildest kind.[5]

This obscurity should not be surprising in Machiavelli's country, where some centuries ago 'the necessity of recurrent terrorism' in order to maintain power was discussed (Discorsi sulla prima deca di Tito Livio, III, I). Looking at a smoke-screen, every narrator of these stories is at least a little conscious that he is walking on eggshells, and shares to some degree the words of Niels Bohr (the father of the renunciation of commonplace world reality in atomic physics): 'Whatever I say must always be considered a question and never a statement'.

MORALISTS AND POLITICIANS

In Italy terrorism has been reduced enormously by many factors, from penetration of the terrorist ranks to substantial reduction in prison terms for people who agree to collaborate with the authorities. Speaking about the Italian case, Laqueur observes rightly that 'Terrorist movements do not have an unlimited life span. If they realize after a few years that the murder of a few politicians (and many innocents) has not brought them any nearer to the target, their resolve weakens'.[6] Table 5.1 below gives a general idea of the terrorist trend in Italy.

Terrorism experts say that a new trend in international terrorism is the birth of a generation of people characterized by less education or moral involvement. This may be true, but from an historical point of view the politics of fear originating in Italy in the late 1960s was connected with the eternal questions about 'what people are and

Table 5.1

Year	Number of terrorist assaults	Number of assaults in which people died or injured		
			Dead	Injured
1969	398	3	19	88
1970	376	2	7	50
1971	539	2	2	0
1972	595	3	5	2
1973	426	5	40	61
1974	573	7	26	199
1975	702	14	10	7
1976	1353	13	10	6
1977	1926	45	13	34
1978	2379	67	35	54
1979	2513	66	24	101
1980	1502	48	125	236
1981	634	34	25	16
1982	347	17	23	42
1983	156	11	10	3
1984	85	6	20	134
1985	63	11	20	146
1986	24	3	2	2
1987	8	2	3	0

Source: the Interior Ministry, and *Corriere della sera*, 25 January 1988

what people ought to be'.[7] The diversities of left- and right-wing motivations are great, but they have in common this kind of distorted and bloody idealism known to all who have studied the problem sufficiently. It is enough to remember the classical words pronounced during 'The Reign of Terror' by Robespierre and Saint-Just about the necessity of linking virtue and terror.[8]

The first Italian episodes of terrorism were not a product of a revolution of rising expectations or of the 'all and now' culture, but a utopian and tragic prefiguration of a future society, where human behaviours would be guided by principles like 'From each according to his ability, to each according to his needs'. Frequently, a rigid morality and a social-conscious mentality led to political commitment, and a total personal involvement was identified with the legitimation of terror.

From a juridical point of view, we must distinguish between

the guilty act (*actus reus*) and the guilty mind (*mens rea*). From a sociological point of view, we can see both the limitations of 'social cause theories' applied to terrorism, and the necessity to understand (in German, *Verstehen*) terroristic events as *actions*, perpetrated in a web of social meanings and relations. Structural predispositions and individual propensities are juxtaposed in terrorist actions, which like other kinds of actions are highlighted by peculiar beliefs about what is morally right to desire: a moral world is a human necessity. In the multiplicity of moral worlds, the relationship between ethics and politics is also a relationship between goals and means; for moral absolutists, what matters is always the goal; and the means, however objectionable to conventional morality, may still be justified by the goal. Casuistry did not help the moral absolutists: they believed in the supreme mastery of their ethical schemes and were prepared to sacrifice other lives and often their own for the sake of the supreme goal. In their kangaroo courts acts of violence perpetrated against 'enemies' were justified by the 'morality' of the end.

Some moral absolutists came from Marxist–Leninist organizations, others from a militancy in the fascist right, and yet others from more traditional Catholic backgrounds. All grew within political groups which were equipped with ideologies that legitimize 'armed insurrection against the powers of the state'. Unconscious supporters of terrorism are the people who permit the worst interpretation of those ideologies which admit both pacific change and change through violence.

It is possible to interpret Leninism in many ways: the terroristic way is possible, but another way is philologically possible too. An emphasis on morality particular to Bolshevik theory is part of stresses that morality is completely subservient to the interests of the revolution. A vanguard of professional revolutionaries speaks in the name of the proletariat and holds power in trust for it; what always matters is the goal, and the means are justified by the goal. In October 1920 Lenin defined 'communist ethics' in opposition to morality of the bourgeoisie,

> who declared that ethics were God's commandments. We do not believe in God. . . . We say that our morality is entirely subordinate to the interests of the class struggle of the proletariat. . . . For the communist, morality consists entirely of compact united discipline and conscious mass struggle against the exploiters.

In Leninist doctrine it is also possible to find pages against terrorism, which is rejected because it is considered as a lost contact between the people and the revolutionary party, whose real task is to organize a mass revolutionary movement. In some ways, Leninism could seem Janus-faced. In Leninist doctrine one can find sentences like: 'The experience of the entire history of the Russian revolutionary movement warns us against such methods of struggle as terrorism';[9] and Leninist statements about the impossibility of rejecting terror in principle.

Many observers of Italian terrorism have stressed that sources of and responsibility for terrorism are to be found in the institutional left (which bred terrorist children), in the university professors (who distorted), in the intellectual establishment (which glamorized), in the press (which printed sensational and horrendous histories). We shall return to these problems later when we speak about the perceptions of Middle-East terrorism in Italy today.

Terrorism is also a paradox of morality and a state of mind, but the dismissal of deterrence would be far too cavalier. Raising the cost of terrorism results in less terrorism. The calculus between the costs and rewards could have liquidated quickly the crusade of the moralists. The protest against the philistinism of the world could have taken many paths, and it is questionable why the terroristic path was so easy to walk.

The anti-terrorist legislation of 1979–80, which offered indulgent sentences to terrorists who co-operated with the investigators, marked the turning point in the history of Italian terrorism: it was the beginning of a series of revelations, infiltrations, arrests and trials which resulted in the definitive ruin of extremist organizations. The anti-terrorist legislation of 1979–80 arrived after many other vain attempts to find the right measures to combat the increasing wave of terrorism.

Above all, the political class was accused of both incapacity and complicity. These allegations were formulated not by leftist and radical opponents, but by conservative or moderate observers like judges of the High Court of Appeal in Milan, who wrote in one opinion:

The legislature, for complicity with political power, after having ignored for years or having tolerated the growth of leftist terrorism and its underground connections with that of the right and with organized crime, woke up only when terrorism had surpassed any bearable limit. These limits were unbearable not by the State but by the politicians in power. Terrorism became unbearable when it started to strike at 'the heart of the State', with which the politicians identified themselves.[10]

These kinds of allegations of incapacity and collusion on the part of the political class have been frequent; Judge Spataro, who for years has had to do with terrorist trials, stated in an Italian newspaper:

It has been found out that a certain political party supported the reasons of a certain terrorist prisoner when he promised revelations that would have backed its political theses . . .; while another party took an interest in the situation of other terrorist prisoners when they promised to hand over documents and other secret materials that would have given new light on particular matters. Some prisoners even, when they changed their own orientations, passed simultaneously from the orbit of a certain political party to the orbit of another one. . . . And sometimes all of this happened in a competitive atmosphere, as if it were essential for some politicians to attract the prisoners to their own area of interest and discussion, and thus taking them away from other areas. Of course the search for a good image had its importance, and consequently a race to appear more receptive and more far-sighted began.[11]

There are many kinds of allegations against the political class, and there are of course answers from the political class rejecting every responsibility. For instance, the Parliamentary committee on the pseudo-Masonic lodge P2 stated 'the P2 lodge is seriously implicated in the Italicus massacre and can be considered even responsible in historical and political (not legal) terms, because it was an essential economic, organization/and moral cradle of it'. The committee stated in formal terms that the P2 lodge was responsible for the hidden direction of terrorism, and that the P2 lodge was not 'a child of the party system'. The majority of the committee ended its work with an allusive invitation to 'an interpretation not restricted to narrow domestic horizons': the big shoulders of superpowers were considered strong enough to bear the load of felonious and unproven charges.

Classical political thinkers from Aristotle to Cicero, including Machiavelli, have said that the best human virtues express them- selves in the political sphere. The political class is not a homogeneous reality, and the attempt to place responsibility elsewhere was too evident. Many other minority reports contradicted the interpretation of the majority, signed by Christian Democrats, Communists, Socialists, Republicans, and other smaller forces. Outspokenly, the representative M. Teodori wrote in his minority report:

> My interpretation of the P2 lodge is opposed to that of the majority of Parliamentary members belonging to other political parties. In their opinion, the P2 lodge was something alien to the party system; in my opinion, each specific fact proves that 'P2ists' and politicians have worked closely in order to illegally manage power. In their opinion, Communists and Christian Democrats were the victims of the P2 lodge; in my opinion, they were, with factions of other parties, the accomplices.[12]

THE 'STRATEGY OF TENSION'

In Italy the term 'strategy of tension' has been used to refer to the hypothesis of an organized conspiracy which inspired the long list of massacres since the bombing of Piazza Fontana on 12 December 1969, where thirteen people were killed and ninety wounded.[13] The conspiracy was supposedly intended to cause intimidation, fear and apprehension in order to conserve the status quo in Italy, and to prevent the co-opting of the communist party into the governmental area. Terrorism and massacres have been considered the result of a plot involving elements of the Italian secret services and the far right.

The roots of this hypothesis are in the great political problems of Italy. After the fall of fascism, the authoritarian tendency within the country was still strong; the fear of communism anguished many sectors of Italian society which was, in some respects, very traditional. In the late 1960s the backward sector of Italian elites looked appreciatively towards the possibility of giving a reactionary answer to the social and political problems resulting from the so-called 'modernization' of the country (massive student demonstrations, legalization of divorce and abortion, rise of the unions, and so on). Italian politics, from the beginning of the 1960s, was frequently haunted by the obsession of a 'Salazar-type regime'. But, when the right alternative was attempted, it ended up with an 'opening to the left'. The increasing tendency to the left culminated in the mid-1970s: after the serious setbacks of the Christian Democrats in the local elections of June 1975, in the electoral campaign of 1976 the communist share of the vote jumped to two percentage points behind the majority party.

At the centre of the Italian case there is the institutional frame of the political system. The Italian constitution (written immediately after the fall of fascism) had been written in fear of a one-party-dominated political structure. The founding fathers of the Italian republic were so frightened by the experience of fascism that they preferred to draw up a formula based on the proportional system. In a highly fragmented parliament, large coalitions are always necessary in order to elect the cabinet, and large majorities are necessary for most of the legislative procedures, thereby weakening the executive and creating a powerful legislature. The vulnerability of cabinets and the influence (direct or indirect, for instance the power of veto) of the communist party are consequences of this original sin of the Italian republican system. During the 1950s and 1960s the communists augmented slowly, but after the great social mobilization of the late 1960s the 'red scare' accelerated significantly.

The victory of left-wing forces at the referendum on divorce and the gains of PCI at the local election of 1975, later confirmed at the general elections of the following year, and the proposal of the 'historical compromise' between catholics and communists dramatically boosted apprehensions. A communist as President of the Chamber and communists holding a quarter of the chairmanships in the Chamber and Senate committees were just some results of the general elections of 1976.

In the opinion of some observers, a strategy of tension has accompanied this increase of communist influence in the governmental area. The tension was intended to be a means to intimidate both the politicians and the electorate. The Italian secret services should have been in some way 'deviated' by people who tried to oppose the strong rise of the Italian Communist Party and the ambiguous disposition of the DC, which in some way was forced to seek arrangements in all the directions and, on the other hand, preferred an under-the-table deal with the communists in order to conserve power.

In G. Galli's opinion, from the beginning of the leftist armed struggle until the liberation of General Dozier the Italian secret services were neither unprepared nor misinformed. They replied to leftist terrorism only when they believed it convenient to do so. They made possible many terrorist initiatives, but stopped them when the true goal was obtained, which was the containment of the Italian communists and the crisis of the incorporation of the PCI into the governmental area. In this way an invisible and international anti-communist organization (which controlled or influenced Italian and foreign secret services) promoted stabilization by destabilization. From this point of view, right-wing – secret services collusion dates back to the early 1960s and from the beginning terrorism was handled by forces like the pseudo-Masonic lodge P2.

Obviously, this interpretation is vehemently rejected by people who have responsibility of the secret services. They stress that delays and errors in effect did take place, but claim that these were often due to factors outside their control. The students' protest shifted with great velocity from pacific demonstrations to urban guerrilla warfare, and this caused basic intelligence failures. Delays and errors were not calculated; at the beginning of terrorism, the secret services were in the early stages of developing counter measures. The head of the Italian police, who is the greatest authority on these problems, asserted: 'in a phase characterized by the incapacity of the apparatus, credit has been given to personages without an institutional role, but who, in spite of that, have never assumed an important part in recent Italian history'.[14] Concerning the existence of a national and international network of complicity, he has stated:

> Existence of foreign-state complicity does not result, but connections certainly existed with foreign terrorist groups. Due to the state-apparatus loyalty, it is difficult to express a general absolutory statement; but it can be stated that deliberate acts of violation and damage to national interests did not take place; if they did, the subjects who perpetrated them acted outside the administration as bearers of illegal interests.[15]

Also the Italian intelligence community is not a homogeneous reality.

The interpretation given by the security services contrasts with the interpetration given by the Permanent Parliamentary Commission for the Control of the Security System, and with the interpetration given by some examining magistrates,[16] who have investigated the many massacres that characterize the history of Italian terrorism. Of particular importance is the interpetration given by the examining magistrates who investigated the massacre on 2 August 1980 in Bologna, where 85 were killed, and 200 wounded. These magistrates supported the hypothesis of an international conspiracy connected with big shots and sentenced people who were placed in high positions within the Italian secret services. The judgement referred to an attempt at diversion by high-ranking figures belonging to the secret services, and discovered by the magistrates, who wrote:

> Only the existence of a link of some nature between the authors of the massacre and those who tried to put the investigators on the wrong track can explain such behaviour: either the massacre was executed by the first sent by the others, or the massacre (even independently organized and carried out) was part of a common political plot, which required that the culprits remain undiscovered.[17]

On the same issue, the Court of Appeal has rejected these conclusions, with a second judgement asserting that an attempt at diversion was in fact tried, but in order to take a sum of money which was really stolen. These two different rulings will be followed by a *third and final judgement*.

It is worth underlining that the indictment against what the secret services perpetrated in the past was conducted by magistrates (giving the first judgement), who trusted implicitly the declarations given by the permanent Parliamentary commission for the Control of the Security Services. In fact one can read in their statement: 'The Court comes to the same conclusion as the Parliamentary Commission: there have been facts of very grave degradation and diversion'.[18] The president of the Parliamentary Commission for the Control of the Security Services have defended the first ruling, saying: 'If one says that there has been no plan, if one says that these men were only petty crooks, then it means that one does not want to understand what has happened in Italy in recent years'[19]

Other people (including the magistrates of the second ruling) have condemned the first ruling as misleading and biased; in their analysis it is a comfortable pastiche of theories, hypotheses, details, facts, collected and unified under the same explanation in order to rationalize a staggering amount of criminal events that have been perpetrated over two decades. These polemics are clear signs of the Babel of tongues in discussions of terrorism: the judicial initiatives are often much disputed and there have been cases of indictment of magistrates.

Some observers have high hopes of the newborn Parliamentary Committee 'to evaluate the results of the struggle against terrorism and to examine the causes which have prevented the identification of the culprits of the massacres'. But the first workings of the committee are not auspicious. The President of the Committee (the same person previously at the head of the Permanent Parliamentary Commission for the Control of the Secret Services) stated clamorously at the first appearance on the stage: 'The impression of those who have attempted to penetrate within these mysteries is that the judges and the police have constantly faced a barrage placed by institutional powers high enough to permit itself not to obey them and strong enough to avoid any sanction'.[20] The work of the committee will be difficult and controversial, but very interesting indeed. In a heterogeneous and polycentric Parliament like the present one in Italy, the possibility of reaching univocal conclusions is barred.

THE ANTI-CIA SCHOOL

The more sinister fantasies of the anti-CIA school have found fertile ground in the interpretations of Italian terrorism. In fact the intervention of the USA secret service in Italy has a long history, dating back to the Allied Invasion of Sicily on 10 July 1943. The Allied offensive overwhelmed the fascists, using all the means at its disposal, including connections with the Sicilian mafia and the Italian-American mafia. Compromise with criminals has been an accepted practice throughout all wars, but today this specific compromise is still held up by anti-American moralists[21] as an important precedent with regard to the capability of the USA to stoop to illegal and dangerous agreements for reasons of *realpolitik*.

In the immediate post-war climate of economic hardship and increasing popular unrest, the USA decided to help the Italians choose moderate groups against the communists, who hoped to remake Italy according to the Stalinist idea of 'people's republic' like those established behind the Iron Curtain. As a result of various events during the post-war period, Italy accepted the Marshall Plan, joined NATO, and was governed by a political class closely linked to the USA administrations. 'In retrospect, American involvement in the stabilization of Italy was a significant, if troubling, achievement. American power assured Italians the right to choose their future form of government and also was employed to ensure that they choose democracy'[22]

Covert operations to buttress anti-communist elements in Italian society were performed before the CIA was founded, in September

1947. Afterwards, for many reasons, such as the presence there of a very important communist party and the seat of the Pope, the CIA continued to consider Italy a fragile cornerstone of the western political system. From J. Angleton to W. Colby, the cream of the American Intelligentsia has spent some years of their training in Rome.

Generally speaking, covert actions were judged by Americans to be particularly positive and were often required by Italian allies. During the 1950s many low-risk and high-profile operations were performed by the CIA, for example the overthrowing of Jacobo Arbenz in Guatemala and Mohammed Mossadegh in Iran in the 1950s. But these decisive political outcomes required only a small effort and a little push; in later years the problems and the means used became very different.

As the enthusiasm for covert action grew during the 1950s, disillusionment came as the result of the failures of the Bay of Pigs, Vietnam and Chile. Later, out of the remains of the Watergate affair, a broader debate surfaced within public opinion, regarding the basic values of democratic society, with a tide of sanctimonious comments about the evils of secrecy. The 1970s were characterized by intense scrutiny and public debate over CIA activities – often focusing on problems like assassinations, or pressures against democratically elected governments (efforts against Salvador Allende in Chile ended in the coup in which he died). In 1974 the CIA Director William Colby told Congress the truth about the clandestine operations against the Allende government in Chile; these operations began to be unravelled in public and caused enormous debate. During this unprecedented uproar, many skeletons were brought out of the closets and, above all, the possibility of using the 'dirty tricks' of the past was extremely reduced. The big change arrived when in the mid-1970s almost all intelligence operations became public, sometimes before they were concluded. In 1975 covert actions came to a near halt, because they were considered difficult to control, morally questionable and often producing undesired results. Revelations of widespread abuses led a wrathful Congress to establish intensive investigations. The impact of the Rockefeller Commission on CIA activities within the USA was shocking; the final result of the Church Committee in the Senate and the Pike Committee in the House was to strengthen the congressional hand in policy debates. Above all, this period is the beginning of what the founder of the Association of Former Intelligence Officers has called *the Big Leak*:

> In the past, the US ship of state leaked from the bottom. Now it began to leak, profusely, from the bridge. The Administration, Congress even intelligence agencies, leaked. Sometimes, as in the 'covert' support of Nicaraguan contras it seemed the Administration wanted secrets to leak. The dismal era of overt covert action had begun.[23]

In this situation, it seems difficult to believe that someone in the CIA could have promoted such a risky covert operation as an explicit involvement in Italian terrorism in order to kill hundreds of people, including the major political leader of the country. Another important point is that even if someone had had this brilliant idea, he would have been faced with the resolute hostility of his other colleagues within the CIA. When Jimmy Carter was elected President, he appointed Admiral Stansfield Turner as Director of Central Intelligence. This was the point of view of the new head of the CIA:

> I felt personally responsible for preventing any repetition of the kind of error the old system had failed to prevent. I owed the President the assurance that the old practices would not be revived. He had never specifically stressed 'cleaning up' the CIA to me, but it was clear that he expected high ethical standards from all of us who worked for him. And I owed it to the CIA to keep it out of trouble, for I believed in the CIA's importance and wanted to maintain its usefulness.[24]

This is not rhetoric used after the event, but signals a real confrontation within the apparatus. The antithesis in the CIA was very clear and hard between those who were inclined to continue using unorthodox methods as in the past, and those who preferred to stay within stricter moral and legal limits. In the episode known as 'the Halloween massacre' Admiral Turner reduced the size of the covert operation section from 1,200 to 400 agents, firing 800 'Old Boys', many of them members of the inner club in the Agency.

The importance of these events to the Italian case is connected to the improbability that, during the crisis of the intelligence community,[25] some public American authorities could have taken particularly dramatic initiatives regarding Italy. Of course remarkable attention was given to the Italian labyrinth (and equal attention to what was happening in France, Greece, Portugal, Spain, and so on), and, indeed, analytical and practical activities were being conducted at various levels. But there is a big difference between this and the hypothesis of a sinister conspiracy orchestrated by public American authorities. It is important to underline that from 1976 to 1980, when Italian terrorism was at its height, the USA was ruled by an administration that was for some time the most open and broadminded in relation to an eventual presence of communists in the cabinet. From 1973 the communist party's secretary general proposed to the Italian catholic world a 'historic compromise': both an appeasement between popular forces and a power-sharing agreement with the Christian Democrats. This prospect was viewed with great concern by Kissinger, who together with Sonnenfeld had repeated, in 1975, the necessity of an ultimate defence of the international status quo. Instead, this prospect was judged differently by Carter and Brzezinski[26] who on several occasions in 1975 expressed themselves in a tentative way: the problem of Eurocommunism was seen from a geopolitical point of view more aggressive and unbiased. From these differences of opinion, it was thought that western European Communist parties in power and fully independent of Moscow could represent a great factor of destabilization within the Soviet bloc. Therefore, they would probably be more dangerous for the Soviets than for the Americans. These theories were then shelved by Carter and Brzezinski, but remained as possibilities discussed by many important analysts of the Italian situation.

To summarize: the greatest manifestation of Italian terrorism was during the years in which men like Carter and Turner (accused of being moralistic, liberal, soft and naive strategists), were at the top; years during which the American secret service seemed almost paralysed in regard to the hypothesis of conducting particularly risky and illegal covert operations.[27]

At the end of the Reagan Administration, the internal struggles within the USA intelligence were, again, at the centre of the cyclone because of the Iran–Contras affair, and control problems have been reproposed in the long debate following the discovery of new illegal covert operations, conducted mostly outside the CIA and judged by many as amateurish. With regard to Bob Woodward's book,[28] which concerns the revival of the old guard in the CIA, it has been observed: 'despite some disturbing factual lapses, it is an extremely important book', because 'it lays bare, in a way that no reportage has done before, the power struggle between contending factions – both inside and outside the CIA – for control over the nation's foreign intelligence apparatus'.[29] The American intelligence community, as Epstein describes it, is not homogeneous,[30] but divided into three factions: first, the old-fashioned anti-communist faction; second, the technocratic faction; third, the congressional faction, based on the Senate Select Committee on Intelligence. The so-called technocratic faction, led by the Administrator Stansfield Turner during the Carter years, was accused of transforming the CIA into what many people considered 'a sort of data-processing university with tenured job-holders dedicated to gathering information about allies as well as enemies'. The opposition of the technocratic faction to the covert operations abuse is based on an awareness of the unpredictable consequences of traditional spy stories and on faith in space-based intelligence, satellite photography, signal interceptions, and so on. It is believed that all these high-tech gadgetries, associated with other means, like the manoeuvring of economic devices, professional diplomacy, propaganda, other forms of legal operations, and above all the supervision of educated deductive reasoning, are sufficient to control the most difficult problems going on in the world.

As far as an outsider can ascertain, in this situation, characterized by the preponderance of the technocratic establishment's idea of riskless intelligence activities, it is foolish to believe that there was direct intervention by the American government in the handling of the Moro affair and other cases of Italian terrorism. R. Gardner, the American ambassador to Italy during the worst years of Italian terrorism, in an interview for an Italian newspaper, to the question 'What is your opinion about Moro?', replied:

He was a man of great importance and his friendship honoured me. . . . I consider him a hero. I say this because of a private detail. When the Red Brigades interrogated him, and he was at their mercy, they asked him about our meetings. He could have said who knows what, to take some advantage. If you check the 'reports' of those interrogations, it can be seen that he told the truth: I had shown him the non-interference policy of the Carter administration and our evident and known preferences. I had never raised my voice in even one of our meetings. Moro was a gentleman and a hero.[31]

THE SPECTRE OF COMMUNISM

It is a difficult to suspect the Italian Communist Party (PCI) of terrorism. During the fascist period, Italian communists organized clandestine cells and a clandestine network of resistance to fascism. During the collapse of the dictatorship they organized guerrilla actions and armed clandestine groups. But the choice of an open struggle was the significant aspect of their strategy; they were active above all in the factories of the major northern cities in order to expand propaganda and enroll workers in their party. To many observers today, they are above all normal politicians involved in the co-operative movement, the trade unions, and the guidance of several important regions and municipalities. In brief: they are 'at home in the world of constitutional, pluralist politics'.[32] A certain independence of Soviet influence and the acceptance of a pluralist party system are important characteristics of the communist party. They have been accused of being responsible for terrorism, but only from these points of view: an earlier underestimation of the problem, an exposure on the cycle of protest that developed in Italy during the late 1960s, the cultural peculiarities of Marxism–Leninism (a journalist wrote that the terrorists were like the unwanted children in the 'Family Album' of the left).[33] The PCI was a strong antagonist of terrorism, even if many terrorists claimed that they were just 'Communists' or 'true Communists', opposed to the 'bourgeois Communism' of the PCI.[34]

More suspicions have been raised concerning the involvement of the USSR in Italian terrorism. In 1917 the Bolsheviks triumphed, using terror on various occasions. In September 1918, after the assassination of the chairman of the Petrograd Cheka and the attempted assassination of Lenin, the Soviet cabinet launched 'Red Terror'. In building the Soviet state, the secret police had a very important role as an instrument of social control. In many points of its history, the USSR has been accused of being a totalitarian state, ruled by terror and exporting this beyond its national borders. The ideology of inevitable class warfare and other aspects of Marxism–Leninism have induced the suspicion that the ultimate goal of the USSR is world domination.

When, on 13 May 1981, Mehemet Ali Agca shot Pope John Paul II in Rome, there was immediate suspicion of the Soviet secret services. Ali Agca was thought to be a drug-runner employed by Bulgaria. As suspicions spread that the shooting was the result of a plot, investigations revealed *probable* involvement of the Bulgarian government, *presumably* with the acquiescence of the KGB. After a long trial, Bulgaria was acquitted of evident responsibility. Apart from the shooting of the Pope, there have been many allegations concerning the responsibility of east European states. In a reconstruction made by M.A. Ledeen there are references to the first-hand testimonies of very important eastern defectors about Soviet and Bulgarian involvement in Italian terrorism; he also exhibits other first-hand evidence of Soviet assistance to terrorists in Europe. In agreement with this analysis, some well-known figures in the Red Brigades were instructed in Czechoslovakia. 'At a minimum, the founders of left-wing Italian terrorism of the sixties went to Prague to meet people experienced in running a clandestine network in Italy'.[35]

These kind of allegations have been confirmed by official statements. On 2 February 1983, after large-scale hearings of the US Senate Subcommittee on Security and Terrorism, the Committee's chairman, Senator Jeremiah Denton, proclaimed: 'The hearings . . . document extensive involvement and complicity by the Soviet Union and its surrogates in a worldwide network of terrorism'.

Nevertheless opinion about USSR involvement is very controversial. For instance, in Bob Woodward's *Veil*, the KGB is sporadically mentioned, except to exonerate it from any involvement in terrorism and above all in the shooting of Pope John Paul II. To the observers this position indicates that the CIA sources who spoke freely and frequently to Woodward no longer consider the Soviets as the worst enemy. There are many indicators of this crucial exoneration.

In a striking revelation, [36] former CIA Director William Casey is shown angrily ordering CIA analysts of terrorism (who were not able to indicate any evidence of links between terrorist groups and the Soviet Union) to read Claire Sterling's book, *The Time of theAssassins*, because they would find much evidence there about these links. But to their disappointment the analysts realized that almost all the proof she cited in her famous book was CIA disinformation, scrupulously planted every so often in the international press and, afterwards, unwittingly used by Ms. Sterling as the plain truth.

Eventual involvement of sectors of the USSR intelligence community (which is not a homogeneous reality) in Italian terrorism has been motivated by an interest in destabilizing the Italian Communist Party. The PCI is the most important communist party outside the Soviet bloc, and its relations with the Soviet

Union are pivotal for many other communist parties and for eastern European states. The strategy of the PCI during the 1970s was characterized by the proposal of a 'historic compromise' with the Christian Democrats. This proposal reflected the lesson given by the fall of the Chilean leftist government of S. Allende – toppled by a military coup supported by foreign intervention. The opposition of Chilean Christian Democrats was essential to the fall of Allende's government, and Berlinguer, the head of the Italian communist party, was cautious about the possibility of repeating the same error. He proposed a 'historic compromise' with the Christian Democrats, and clearly rejected the hypothesis of a revived popular front with leftist forces. In his opinion a broader political base was required for the incorporation of the communist party in the governmental majority. The Italian population, he indicated, must be prevented from 'splitting down the middle into two counterposed enemy camps'.

Berlinguer admitted that the Atlantic Pact was a big pillar for the equilibrium between east and west. Dramatically, he argued that Italy's withdrawal from NATO could have a destabilizing effect, and rejected this proposal. In the opinion of many observers, Berlinguer's ideas were motivated not by the theory that any sudden shift in the balance of forces might imperil the process of *détente*, but by fear of the 'Brezhnev doctrine': once socialist, always socialist. The Kremlin affirmed the right of the leading communist state to intervene in the affairs of others: any satellite which tried to break away could be 'aided' by its socialist brothers. Berlinguer had denounced the Russian invasion of Czechoslovakia and did not want the help of the Russian 'Big Brother'.

The 'Italian path' had already exercised a potent attraction for different communist parties, above all in Yugoslavia, Spain and France. The choice of a peaceful way to socialism and a declaration of independence from Moscow were the opportunity for western communist parties to escape from the political limbo where they would otherwise be condemned to stay for ever. In November 1975, the French communists announced their conversion to Eurocommunism and made an extraordinary effort to distance their party from the PCUS. The departure of the French communist party from Eurocommunism happened later, in a way that has been connected with Italian events.

On 19 March 1978 the French left suffered a narrow but decisive electoral defeat. The communists broke their 'Common Programme of the Left' with the socialist party. To a number of observers the sudden and specious collapse of the 'unity of action' pact had unmistakably revealed that they would rather lose than break off definitively with Moscow. Within the Eurocommunist camp internal divisions were considerable. The philosoviets in the western communist parties, who strongly opposed the Eurocommunist option, preferred a hard-line policy that looked suspiciously like a Soviet interference. The French alliance breakdown seemed a strangely self-defeating choice: a certain electoral fortune was thrown out for no apparent reason. French communists preferred to discredit themselves and suffer for many years a big loss of dissidents and voters (even though having tried unsuccessfully to oppose the decline with various changes of political line). After these events, the French party became again Moscow's most faithful ally in western Europe. To some observers, the explanation of all that the PCF did in 1977 is to be found in the hidden hand of the communist party of the Soviet Union; according to them, the party's secretary general obeyed the Kremlin because he was being blackmailed, due to a compromised wartime past.[37] What happened in France, therefore, highlights what happened in Italy. In no way is it surprising that the Soviets have watched with apprehension the success of the Italian communists; their search for independence had procured many enemies in Moscow and few friends in Washington. R. Aron stated perfectly that the Italian path had 'an equivocal destiny, suspected by all and unable to be successful by itself'.[38] The main characteristic of this interpretation is that it is not founded on the existence of secure documental evidence, but on a prodigious storehouse of deductions and suppositions.[39]

The image of the Soviet Union as 'a riddle, wrapped in a mystery, inside an enigma' has changed a lot in recent years. The Soviet obsession for secrecy invited suspicion that the communists were at the centre of an overall framework of sanctuary, embassies, weapons, money, and training camps. The involvement of the Soviet Union and of some of its satellites was connected with the escalation of US–Soviet rivalry.

In the new Gorbachev era, Soviet intentions, viewpoints and way of thinking are now seen in a less antagonistic light, as previously indicated in scholarly research,[40] and like a hope, not an accusation, it is now possible to read statements such as: 'The danger (of terrorism) cannot be reduced without Soviet co-operation'.[41]

NATIONALISM AND TERRORISM

South-Tyrolian terrorism is a case of terrorism supported and tolerated by a network in part identifiable and visible in a way that can be compared to the IRA in Northern Ireland or to ETA in the Basque country. However, the difference is still huge because this South-Tyrolian terrorism is weak in comparison, and the support for it is even weaker. The problem started in 1919 when Italy took over the South Tyrol, a German-speaking area with an enormous consciousness of its own ethnic specificity. For many years Italian governments have tried unsuccessfully to assimilate this population. Over the years the problem has become an occasion of conflicts and permanent tensions. Since the second World War there have been almost 400 terrorist attempts, and in 1988 there was a remarkable escalation, perhaps stimulated by the electoral campaign that was carried out in a atmosphere of bombings and violence.

Many groups and organizations have been suspected of being supporters of South-Tyrolian terrorism; the most accused one has been *Heimatbund*, a party which obtained 25 per cent of votes in the 1983 elections. This little political party asks in the strongest way for self-determination and aims for the creation of an independent South-Tyrolian state. Other suspected groups are on the right side of the South-Tyrolian Volkspartei (the big party which represents South-Tyrolians in local and national Italian political bodies) and of Schuetzen, (the military corps which is not represented in the elections, and is on extremist positions). It must be said that the Heimatbund party rejects disdainfully these allegations. Its leader, Eva Klotz, daughter of a person sentenced for terrorist activities perpetrated in the 1960s, says:

We want to obtain our goal by pacific means, but Italians always accuse both the Schuetzen and us of planting all the bombs. After each attempt the houses of our group members and supporters are searched, and nothing is ever found. But all of this greatly damages us, both on a moral and on an electoral basis. First, we are against and we condemn every act of violence and secondly because many, even our own members, do not have the courage to come to our demonstrations. Every attempt takes away thousands of votes from us.[42]

The great majority of South-Tyrolians are cautious about eventual self-determination or unification with Austria. The fruit-growers, farmers, businessmen, tourist operators, hotel owners and politicians have benefited from a tremendous amount of Italian money which derives from huge public Italian subsidies. It could be said that the Italian government has tried to buy peace, paying the highest possible price in cash. And in fact the standard of living in South Tyrol is one of the best in the world. It is not true that 'crime does not pay', and unintended consequences of terrorism are evident in South Tyrol.

As always, there are rumours about the manipulation of terrorists; Italian and Austrian secret services are suspected of being involved as supporters or sponsors. Some observers note that no one suspicion is the right one, but a combination may provide the explanation of what really happens in this area. It is still not known whether South-Tyrolian terrorism is a vast organized network or the work of isolated minorities supported by foreign powers. Some outstanding Italian columnists have openly supported the second thesis; for instance, G. Zucconi has written: 'The bombings and attempts which upset Alto Adige in the Sixties terminated when Italy stated clearly to Austria that if it didn't stop sheltering and protecting the bombers, we would have opposed Austrian entrance into the European Community'.[43]

Since the 1950s, the Italian and Austrian governments have argued many times regarding the repression of terrorism. It is interesting that in 1961 the Austrian government asserted that the South-Tyrolian terrorist attempts should have been considered political offences, and moreover affirmed in a note given to the Italian ambassador to Vienna:

the republic of Austria, in the national as well as in the international sphere, adheres unconditionally to the principle of the supremacy of law. All the suspicious facts coming to the knowledge of the Austrian authorities are investigated and prosecuted if the suspected acts are punishable under Austrian law. But in view of well-known international usage and the provisions of Italian law, it is surely a redundancy to specially emphasize that acts committed outside a country for political motives can neither be prosecuted within the country nor can legal assistance be rendered in the prosecution of such acts.[44]

Recently, the Italian and Austrian Ministers of the Interior met and resumed the collaboration between the two countries. After the arrests of some South-Tyrolian terrorists in Austria, an influential Italian newspaper commented: 'These arrests constitute an important signal: for the first time Austria has helped the Italian police and judges who for years had sought collaboration, especially controls over South-Tyrolian suspects and connections with neo-Nazi circles in Austria and in Bavaria'.[45]

Like terrorist events related to ethnic conflict in the border region of South Tyrol, terrorist events related to conflict in the Middle East are supported or tolerated by a network in part visible and identifiable.

After the second World War, the first collaboration between Italians and Arab states began for reasons connected with oil policy: Italian entrepreneurs offered themselves as interlocutors and supporters for economic reasons. The turning point of Italian politics in the Middle East was the autumn of 1973, when, after the Yom Kippur war between Israel and bordering peoples, the price Italy was required to pay for eastern oil increased enormously. Italy was discovered to be particularly vulnerable in the lowest period of its republican history: by mid-decade it ranked as the world's most indebted industrialized nation. After 1973 Italian politics in the Middle East featured the same problem: energy policy is crucial to a country which heavily depends on oil imports (and has recently voted to renounce a nuclear policy).

The tendency to find 'important alliances' on the southern edge of the Mediterranean or in the north of Africa is widespread in the large majority of Italian political class. Some politicians (often bored by legal niceties at the domestic level, which is very frequent in one of the most corrupt political systems of the world) have discovered, for personal ambition or megalomania, a vocation to play a greater and more libertarian role on the international level, and above all in the Mediterranean area – 'our fate for so many centuries!', as they say so emphatically.

Temptation to play an interventionist role in the Mediterranean is also induced by substantial problems, like the oil policy or north Africa's multiplying community. More than 75 per cent of the burgeoning populations of Morocco, Algeria and Tunisia are under 25 years old, and seem mature for religious radicalization. In a Europe which is rediscovering its underclass, the possibility of being surrounded by a ring of very poor, overpopulated and Iran-like Islamic states is a nightmare. The Americans have the same nightmare of a victorious communist revolution in Mexico, with the difference that Europe's nightmare could become reality quite soon.

The Fiumicino Airport attempt of 1973 was the worst in the history of international terrorism in Italy (32 dead, 15 wounded) and it marked the definite turning point in the Italian attitude towards the Palestinian conflict.

This persuaded the then Minister of Foreign Affairs Aldo Moro to promote through Colonel Giovannone, a shrewd easing-off of political action with mid-eastern groups, and this resulted in a long non-belligerent period of Palestinian terrorism in Italy. The characteristic of Arab strategy in Italy was complete autonomy from the uprising of European terrorism.[46]

The search to stipulate a mutual agreement to avoid belligerency in Italy has been a constant trait of Italian foreign policy in the Middle East. Even if some deals with Palestinians and Libyans have occurred, leftist terrorism in Italy remains basically 'Italian terrorism', without great connections with international terrorism. Many observers affirm that this was a great success of Italian secret services.

It has been noted that all governments uniformly offer rhetorical opposition to terrorism. But in fact there are many categories:

A few governments actually *oppose* terrorism, and do so consistently; others actively *support* terrorists; but most fall in to a third broad category, the *neutrals*. They either acquiesce in terrorism or refuse outright to oppose it. A proper policy toward terrorism must take into account each of these types of states.[47]

The answer to this problem needs to be worded carefully. A simple dichotomy between opponents and supporters risks being misrepresentative. A sincere neutral position could be morally repugnant, and in practice hypocritical, but logically conceivable.

The discussions about Article 1 of the second Hague Convention in 1907 and about the United Nations Charter illustrate nevertheless that there is a tension between the idea of neutrality and 'the sentiment of justice'.[48] Acquiescence could indirectly promote further terrorism, and it is absolutely true that he who acquiesces in terrorism could in practice support it. The Italian situation was characterized by the search for a middle ground of non-involvement in the Palestinian drama. Dangerous compromises resulted, but they are different from intentional support for terrorism and do not reflect Italian cabinets and the PLO going to bed together. At the beginning, compromises were above all responses aimed at ending the conflicts on Italian territory; they have sometimes then degenerated into a kind of way to hell paved with good intentions (like in the 'Iran-Contra affair'). It has been recognized that, however well-intentioned, separate deals with state-sponsored terrorism and indulgent treatment of terrorists have occurred. For instance, some observers have denounced freedom of movement and liberation of terrorists in exchange for promises of immunity. It is well known that the problem is international. Some Italian politicians have been charlatans and masters of ambiguity in presenting themselves as dyed-in-the-wool pacifists, and occasionally they have expressed the same kind of gratuitous remarks made by Mr William Waldegrave, British Foreign Office Minister, who asserted that Israel's founding fathers had once been involved 'in what we at the time described as terrorism'. From this point of view, 'since the Israeli Prime Minister, Mr Yitzhak Shamir, and Mr Arafat share the status of reformed terrorists, it is illogical of the one to refuse to parley with the other'.[49]

B. Netanyahu says appropriately that the creation of a common policy on terrorism should be based on two principles: deals with terrorists encourage terrorism everywhere; deterrents work on terrorists just as they do on anyone else. These principles originate a commitment to an inflexible campaign against terrorism's sponsors. 'Terrorism is a phenomenon which tries to evoke one feeling: fear. It is understandable that the one virtue most necessary to defeat terrorism is therefore the antithesis of fear: courage'. Fear and adaptation are words which have been treated in the masterpieces of Italian literature: fear in Manzoni's *The Betrothed*, and adaptation in the ironical and sceptical *The Leopard* by the Sicilian Prince of Lampedusa. Neither have concluded that consequentialist courage is at the centre of the national temperament.

For a long time the Italian parliament has given *de facto* recognition to the PLO, and Italian political leaders have maintained that 'Israel's policy in the occupied territories violates international law and human rights'. There is a very large supportive spectrum for the PLO's moderate strategy: from the Pope to the media, from the bureaucrats to the unions, from the cabinet to the communist opposition, there is almost unanimity, even if with significant nuances and differentiated gradations. Exceptions seem as disturbing as singing flat in a chorus.

Above all the Palestinian uprising in the Occupied Territories has been utilized in a large press campaign which has weakened the ancient sympathy of Italian public opinion towards Israel. Regarding the above-mentioned points, the case of the terrorist suspected of launching a bomb among people, mainly children, who were going to a synagogue in Rome on a Sunday morning of 1983, is particularly instructive. He was later arrested in Greece for other facts connected to terrorist activities, but the leftist Greek administration shamefully opposed the tentative moves of the Italian government to put on trial the person suspected, and has recently released this terrorist, who immediately found refuge in Libya. Many observers have indicated that this has not caused the indignation that should be normal, and this is a key signal to the situation of public opinion in Italy regarding the conflict in the Middle East. Putting aside allegations against the Italian government that they did not fully and quickly commit the duties related to the application for extradition from Libya,[50] the inattentiveness of the media is particularly relevant, and deserves some observations about the possibility that omission and misleading information could be considered as acquiescence in terrorism and an indirect support for it.[51]

The problems connected with misleading information, neglect or justification of terrorism have been underlined in the past by many scholars. For instance, La Palombara says: 'terrorism would not have proceeded as far as it did were it not for a certain amount of legitimacy it extracted not only from intellectuals but, through them, from the broader community as well'.[52] Rome's Chief Rabbi Elio Toaff has imputed recent acts and threats of violence against Italian Jews to a new anti-Semitic trend growing in Italy, primarily sustained by Catholic journals and magazines. The country was previously known for its lack of support for the Gestapo; now it is possible to denounce several journals and magazines for poisonous articles, fanning hostility toward Jews, and for lack of distinction between Israelis and Jews. He added that

> while the Vatican itself refrains from directly condemning Israel, it effectively abets the editorial policy of the offending periodicals ... the attacks cannot have escaped the notice of the Vatican, and therefore may fairly be seen as having its tacit consent.[53]

In fact the position of many Catholics is simply astonishing: Christian religious people have been involved in the past in the provisions of arms to terrorists (the Monsignor H. Capucci case).

To many observers a correct understanding of the unconscious cultural support and tolerance of terrorism is missing in Italy today, and this is very dangerous. Recent overtures from the Soviet Union and from the USA are signals of increasing concerted effort by the superpowers to settle the Palestinian conflict. In such a violent and volatile area, conclusions are often ephemeral. The Palestinian conflict has never overflowed to jeopardize the stability of the international society, and internal divisions in the Islamic world are a volcano which has just started to smoke. Probably other tensions will erupt in the future, and the threat of terrorism coming from this area will not end with public recognition of the state of Israel.

MAFIA AND NARCO-TERRORISM

In late nineteenth-century Europe the manufacture of dynamite was seen as a great and disturbing advancement for a terrorist threat then still under age. Panic was caused by the new technology in the hands of dangerous people.[54] Today, the potential threat of nuclear terrorism and of narco-terrorism is comparable to the invention of dynamite, but with a difference: nuclear terrorism, or chemical terrorism, are hypotheses for nightmare scenarios, while narco-terrorism is a reality. The availability of astronomic sums of money provides an infernal chance for this new kind of terrorism, motivated not by ideological or nationalist reasons, but by a simple greed for felony and bullying. The fantastic growth in the sale and use of drugs during the 1970s and 1980s has eclipsed the old mafia, which is now replaced by more coldblooded and less scrupulous drug lords – who use terrorism if it works.

In Italy there is no evidence of the emergence of a narco-terrorist network characterized by continuous relationships with Soviet and eastern European states. It has been proved that some people in Middle-Eastern and eastern European states have ties with international drug dealing groups, but these activities do not seem to be systematically connected with terrorist groups in the European arena.

On this subject, the evaluation relies on legal proceedings in the courts (which in their turn rely on the government service occupied in gathering secret information) rather than on univocal interpretable evidence. A significant example is a trial held in Bari against Italian citizens and foreigners accused of 'organized crime specialized in the traffic of drugs'.[55] The criminal organization was divided in two parts: the Italian part was led by a previous offender, who conducted heroin-trafficking operations which involved several Syrian VIPs, including important generals. According to the Italian judicial inquiry, the leader of the Syrian part of the criminal organization was an officer of the Damascene secret services. His job, supposedly, was that of buying arms and paying for them with the profits made from drugs. Many clues indicated that the heroin traffic was arranged by him, but he was supported by the Damascene government.[56] Before being arrested in Bari, it was believed that he had relations with the Jordanian terrorist who, on 17 April 1986, placed a bomb in his Irish girlfriend's bag, when she was departing on an El Al flight from London.

In the thousands of pages covering the trial, there are indications of the use of heroin as an exchange good in paying for arms destined to be employed in international terrorism. The involvement of Syrian personnel both in the trafficking of heroin and in terrorist arms trade has been denounced by the judges, who have also censured the surprising American connection with the traffickers. It was impossible to conclude an important part of the trial, concerning the relations between the principal Italian suspect and an under-secretary of the Italian finance department, who had written a letter of recommendation for the principal Italian suspect to the Syrian government. There exists, in fact, a peculiar Italian law which stipulates the necessity of an authorization in order to proceed against a parliamentary member who is on the bench of the accused. In this case (and it is worth underlining that cases of this kind happen frequently), parliament has not authorized the investigation into the possibility that the member was implicated in protecting the offender (who was sentenced to 18 years imprisonment in the first judgement, reduced to 14 years by the Court of Appeal). The existence of very friendly relations between the parliamentary member and the offender were however recognized.

This event has distinctive importance because it reveals very well what a deleterious plot of criminal activities grows around drug traffic. The extense of complicity, for 'these big-time gangsters who kill with abandon and evade taxes by the billion', becomes greater and greater because of the colossal earnings of this kind of trade.

Very often, organized crime groups exchange favours. For example, in an important trial in Palermo the involvement of right-wing terrorists in the killing of the Sicilian Regional President is being discussed. The murder is believed to have been commissioned by the mafia and executed by rightist terrorists. Some criminal groups choose purposely to dress up as terrorists and to use terrorist methods. According to judges, one of the many Italian massacres (the so-called 'Christmas massacre': 15 dead, 230 wounded, 23 December 1984) was directly organized by the mafia in order to force the state machinery to move from the battle against the mafia towards the one against terrorism.

In addition to the massacres and bombings used as an efficient political weapon, organizations belonging to the mafia in the course of their illegal trade operate at the centre of an enormous criminal circuit, which has domestic and international tentacles. These organizations have relations with terrorist groups, high-level politicians and equivocal businessmen who work in laundering and recycling dirty money. The head of the Italian police stated:

> In such an entangled situation terrorist acts of great emotional impact are committed, actions which have the immediate consequence of inducing the judges, the police, the anti-mafia Commissioner, the intelligence services to deviate every investigative effort to other fields, conceding in this way a large relief to organized crime.[57]

The mafia, other forms of organized crime (the 'Ndrangheta in Calabria, the Camorra in Campania, divided into many rival groups), ordinary criminality, fragments of the extreme right, fragments of the extreme left, sectors 'diverted' from various state apparatus, pseudo-Masonic associations, other international criminal organizations, and illegal economic groups, constitute already a very vast and dangerous domain governed by people who do not escape from the systematic use of terrorist methods.[58]

When the Prohibition era was drawing to a close, Walter Lippmann wrote:

> The fact that the underworld breaks the law which we all respect in principle, that it employs methods, such as bribery, *terrorism*, and murder, which we all deeply deplore, should not divert our attention from the main point, which is that the underworld performs a function. . . . The underworld, as I am using the term, lives by performing the services which convention may condemn and the law prohibit, but which, nevertheless, human appetites crave.[59]

During the Prohibition era these 'functions' were the supplying of liquor, prostitution, gambling and drugs. The activities of the underworld required lawbreakers, bribery and coercion; yesterday, the same as today, bootlegging and racketeering were operated with the collusion of those in the high sphere of politics. The activities of organized crime, subjected to no law, pervaded by swindle and treachery, always seek protection and complicity among public powers. The big difference between yesterday and today is that the amount of money is now so tremendous that often relations with public powers have both increased and dramatically changed.

The interpenetration between the mafia and key sectors of political power was a distinctive attribute of the Sicilian mafia. In the past the mafioso has seen himself as a 'man of order' rather than a criminal.[60] What distinguished the old mafia[61] from ordinary criminality was the network of connections with institutional power, and the specific setting which was subordinate to it. Now there is such a fantastic amount of money involved that politicians are sometimes accomplices and often, indeed, modest employees. A signal of these changes was the unusual wave of mafia violence which exploded in Sicily in the late 1970s. The victims were high-ranking public figures: police officers, journalists, politicians, magistrates; in the past the old mafia was careful not to hit these targets. The main interest of the new mafia has shifted from real-estate speculation and public works contracts to drug traffic. In southern Italy the recruits of the drug lords did not come from the traditional peasant communities, but from the underclass living in the slums of the old city or in the peripheral public-housing projects, which look like the Third World's lurid shantytowns.[62] The drug traffic grows in this bleak landscape of economic indigence and social collapse: 'a vicious circle of precarious employment, inadequate housing and sanitary facilities, malnutrition, disease, and illiteracy'.[63]

The western institutions have never before confronted this situation: massive crime, massive corruption, massive challenges to the police dealing with foreigners. Not from a liberal point of view, but for economic and social reasons, many observers have proposed a risky social experiment: ending prohibition on drugs.[64] *The Economist*, which argued authoritatively that the government are fighting a losing battle and that they should legalize drugs, stated:

> We do not think that today's prohibition will end within, say, five or ten years. But it is hard to believe, 30 or 40 years from now, governments will still be sending more policemen on to the city streets disguised as drug pushers, training more sniffer

dogs, stopping more aircraft and boats, doing more spot checks at customs posts.

Sooner or later, prohibition will end. For those who can see that, the alternative to present politics is clear: legalise, control, discourage.[65]

This problem to our topic is relevant because the more drugs trafficked, the more potential there is for terrorism and organized crime. G. Falcone, the best-known mafia fighter in Italy, to the question 'does the mafia have support in high political circles in Rome?', replied:

> There is no kind of broad link. There are no organic ties between the mafia and the national power leadership. There have been many attempts to control some politicians – by offering them electoral support in return for favors – but this doesn't mean the mafia enjoys support at the national level. The links between the mafia and politicians are much more subtle than direct. That makes them harder to prove.[66]

These 'subtle links' could be disturbing to investigate. It is well known that all over the world drug traffic develops the most serious network, where you can find bankers and terrorists, innumerable street hustlers and some of the most prominent leaders (for instance, the Justice Minister and the chief federal prosecutor not, as it happened, in the backward south of Italy but in overaffluent and overcivilized Switzerland).

The new potency of organized crime has modified the place of terrorism in Italian society. At the beginning of 1989, C. De Mita, president of the Italian Minister's Council, stated in his six-monthly Parliamentary report on the secret services' activities that the menace of terrorism continues to decrease but organized crime is spreading and today represents 'the principal threat to all institutions'.[67] From another point of view, this new dimension of organized crime has been remarked on by D. Sica, the anti-mafia Commissioner, who has greatly enlarged the hypothesis previously presented by the Head of the Italian police. According to Sica's analysis, in recent years terrorism has become weaker and weaker, but bloody attempts, anonymous or with false labels of terrorism, have been perpetrated by criminal organizations in order to mobilize all the investigators in the war against vanishing terrorists, offering in this way a greater freedom to the activities of the delinquents.

With this crucial evaluation about the new frontier of public alarm, one episode closes and a new hunting ground for ghost-hunters and monster-catchers opens.

FICTION AND NON-FICTION LITERATURE

The literature concerning Italian terrorism is dominated by a culture of suspicion, betrayal and deceit. Italian and foreign secret services have been placed in the dock on the basis of data frequently selected from a slanted point of view. Terrorists have been presented as puppets of the USA or the USSR; in this vision, nations always perform according to the script on the international stage with the superpowers watching threateningly over their shoulders.

From a sociological point of view, in the scene all the actors are puppets, but not blindly dancing on strings of which they are unaware and over which they have no control.[68] Actors are not condemned to the role laid down by the script; there is a reciprocal dependence on power relations and actors have the liberty and opportunity to change the script or to rewrite it. The recital is the result of many factors, including enigmatic behaviour, bounded rationality, and unintended consequences. In the intricate history of Italian terrorism it is very hard to discuss the causes of phenomena with rigorous criteria, and to respect the essential distinction between personal responsibility and institutional responsibility, personal abuses and institutional rules. It is too simple to conceive of terrorism as an independent variable producing death and fear; and it is perhaps deceptive to conceive of terrorism as a dependent variable, strongly or weakly related to a multitude of other variables.

While the academic study of terrorism seems to be settling into specialized patterns of scholarly inquiry, the general literature on terrorism is becoming increasingly characterized by the appearance of a new reader: the reader of mass-market books on intelligence stories. This reader is dissatisfied with the news that appears in the daily press and from official sources, and is searching for exciting truths buried within the tabernacles of the intelligence agencies. There is 'a perennial demand for fictional, factional, semi-fictional, and non-fictional accounts';[69] traditional publishing firms edit books characterized by ever more nightmarish and far-reaching conclusions, which are also sometimes manifestly wrong, sometimes misleading, and sometimes verging on a contribution to abysmal demonology.

W. Laqueur develops a fine comparison between intelligence fiction and intelligence non-fiction. Intelligence fiction (for example the glamorous fantasies of Ian Fleming) does not mirror the realities of intelligence life. In this kind of literature, boring subjects and crucial questions are avoided, and the problems are often depicted in a manichean way. It is not realistic or 'mimetic', to use the classical Aristotelian term which refers to the capacity of a masterwork to mirror reality. However, Laqueur observes:

a substantial part of intelligence nonfiction also is not mimetic but takes very considerable liberties with reality. Some of the reasons are obvious: The fog of uncertainty is frequently difficult to penetrate; reality is often unexciting; a great deal of ingenuity and daring may go into operations that produce little or nothing of real significance. . . . All this is dispiriting. The men and women of intelligence may be not able to do anything about it, but the authors can make their choice if reality is unexciting – hence the embellishment, the selective treatment, the squeezing of facts, and so on. . . . But there is an important difference: science fiction does not aspire to be anything but science fiction, whereas not a few of the allegedly documentary books on intelligence are moving from fact to fiction and back, changing from one literary genre to another in a way of which Aristotle would not have approved, and which, though occasionally entertaining, is bound to cause confusion and distortion.[70]

Are confusion and distortion a by-product of the literature about Italian terrorism? Is this literature nurtured on a diet of spy literature, where the heart of the matter is the theme of betrayal; the same powerful factor which dominates the novels that are regarded as masterpieces by spy fans? Books of this kind are the realm of double agents, dark paranoia and invisible conspiracy.[71]

F. Imposimato, at present a senator elected to the communist party, who in the past was the examining magistrate in the Aldo Moro case, stated: 'In the Moro affair many precise facts are known, which can not be cancelled by the obtusity of mysteriologists . . . They have contributed in creating in the public opinion a sense of dismay, of frustration and of indiscriminate suspicion which is in contrast with the historical truth'. To the question 'Who was behind the Red Brigades?', Imposimato replied: 'The Red Brigades were behind the Red Brigades'.[72]

In the grim history of Italian terrorism, what can instead be assumed is that domestic and international groups of assassins have operated effectively to seek complicity in the highest spheres of political and bureaucratic powers. But this does not authorize either the confusion between loyal security agents and terrorist supporters, or between some disloyal conspirators and the great majority of those who, within the national institutions, acted (and sometimes died) while fulfilling their duties. Trapped in the web we ourselves have spun, to discredit legitimate institutions is the same as discrediting loyalty and obedience to law. This has been an insidious message for the would-be terrorist; from this point of view, what we can at least do is to contain the damage.

NOTES

1   LaPalombara, J. *Democracy Italian Style*, New Haven: Yale University, Press, 1987, p. 180; a book full of optimism, as the author has instructed himself to be almost always benevolent (even about things that others find disturbing). LaPalombara shares the viewpoint of Orson Welles in *The Third Man*: 'Look at Italy under the Borgias. Only warfare, terror, bloodshed, and Michelangelo. In Switzerland they had brotherly love and five hundred years of peace. What did that produce? The cuckoo clock.'

2   Wieviorka M., *Sociétés et terrorisme*, Paris: Fayard, 1988, p. 177 (the translations of all the quotations from French and Italian texts are by F. Sidoti).

3   For a general prospect on the subject, see R.H. Shultz and R. Godson, *Dezinformatsia: Active Measures in Soviet Strategy*, Virginia: Pergamon, 1984.

4   For an examination of the activity of these parliamentary committees, see F. Sidoti, 'Mafia e Parlamento', *Queste Istituzioni*, 71, 1987: 59–77.

5   A typical intellectual fad is to overemphasize the applicability of one's own theory. This has been formulated as *the law of the instrument*: 'give a small boy a hammer, and he will find that everything he encounters needs pounding'. See A. Kaplan, *The Conduct of Inquiry*, San Francisco: Chandler Publishing Co., 1964, p. 29.

6.   W. Laqueur, 'Reflections on Terrorism,' *Foreign Affairs*, October 1986, p. 95.

7.   See Acquaviva, S.S., *Guerriglia e guerra rivoluzionaria in Italia*, Milano: Rizzoli, 1979; G. Statera, ed., *Violenza politica e violenza sociale nell 'Italia degli anni 70*, Milano: Angeli 1983.

8.   Bonanate, L., 'Terrorismo e governabilità', *Rivista Italiana di scienza politica*, XIII, 1982, 1, pp. 37–64.

9.   Lenin, V.I., *Collected Works*, Moscow: Progress Publishers, 1964, vol. 8, p. 22.

10. Quoted in G. Galli, *Storia del partito armato*, Milano: Rizzoli, 1986, p. 145.
11. *Corriere della sera*, 28 January 1988.
12. M. Teodori, *P2: la controstoria*, Milan: SugarCo, 1986, pp. 7–8. Other interesting observations in the minority reports of A. Bastianini and of A. Ghinami, *Commissione parlamentare d'inchiesta sulla Loggia massonica P2*, Camera dei Deputati – Senato della repubblica, IX legislatura, Doc. XXIII no.2–bis/5, Doc.XXIII, n.2–bis/4, Rome, 1984.
13. Anon., *Strage di stato*, Milan: Samonà e Savelli, 1970.
14. Statement made by prefetto V. Parisi, *Commissione parlamentare d'inchiesta sul terrorismo in Italia e sulle cause della mancata individuazione dei responsabili delle stragi*, Rome: Tipografia del Senato, 14 December 1988, p. 32.
15. Statement made by prefetto V. Parisi, 6 December 1988, p. 100.
16. In the Italian legal system, examining magistrates have very important powers, for example the power to conduct detailed investigations, call in witnesses, issue indictments, pronounce sentences and issue warrants for temporary or extended arrest.
17. AA. VV., *La strage. L'atto di accusa dei qiudici di Bologna*, Roma: Editori Riuniti, 1986, p. 281.
18. Documents, excerpts and confrontations between the two sentences are in 'Servizi segreti e strutture clandestine. La ricostruzione giudiziaria del Supersismi', *Questione qiustizia*, 1, 1987, pp. 121–92.
19. *L'espresso*, 30 March 1986.
20. Gualtieri, L., *Relazione alla Commissione parlamentare d'indagine*, Roma: Dattiloscritto, 30 November 1988, p. 1.
21 See S. Haseler, *The Varieties of Anti-Americanism*, Washington, D.C.: Ethics and Public Policy Center, 1985.
22 J.E. Miller, *The United States and Italy, 1940–1950: The Politics and Diplomacy of Stabilization*, Chapel Hill: The University of North Carolina Press, 1986, p. 274.
23 Atlee Phillips, D., 'The CIA, Covert and Overt, Always Survives Its Critics', *Los Angeles Times*, 18 October 1987, Part V, p. 3.
24 Turner, S., *Secrecy and Democracy*, New York: Harper 1986, p. 187.
25 See J. Ranelagh, *The Agency: The Rise and Decline of the CIA*, New York: Simon and Schuster, 1986.
26 For a good reconstruction of this different perspective, see R. Brancoli, *Gli USA e il PCI*, Milan: Garzanti, 1976; R. Brancoli, *Spettatori interessati*, Milan: Garzanti, 1980; M. Margiocco, *Stati Uniti e PCI*, Bari: Laterza, 1981.
27 About some of these issues see E.W. Lefever and R. Godson, *The CIA and American Ethic: An Unfinished Debate*, Washington, D.C.: Ethics and Public Policy Center, 1980; E.W. Lefever, ed., *Morality and Foreign Policy: A Symposium on President Carter's Stance*, Washington D.C.: Ethics and Public Policy Center, 1977.
28 Woodward, Bob, *Veil: The Secret Wars of the CIA*, New York: Simon & Schuster, 1987.
29 Epstein, E. Jay, 'Woodward keeps "Veil" over the political agenda of his own CIA sources', *The Washington Times*, 12 October 1987, p. E7.
30 *See* F. Kaiser, 'Secrecy, Intelligence, and Community: The US

Intelligence Community', in S.K. Tefft, *Secrecy: A Cross-Cultural Perspective*, New York: Human Sciences Press, 1980.
31 *L'espresso*, 27 March 1988.
32 Putnam, R.D., 'The Italian Communist Politician', in D.L.M. Blackmer and S. Tarrow, eds., *Communism in Italy and France*, Princeton, New Jersey, 1975; on the same subject see R. Evans, *Coexistence: Communism and its Practice in Bologna, 1945–1965*, South Bend, Ind.: University of Notre Dame Press, 1967; A. Ranney and G. Sartori, *Eurocommunism: The Italian Case*, Washington, D.C.: The American Enterprise Institution, 1978; and G. Sartori, *Teoria dei partiti e caso italiano*, Milan: SugarCo, 1982.
33 D. Della Porta and S. Tarrow, 'Unwanted children: Political Violence and the Cycle of Protest in Italy', *European Journal of Political Research*, 14, 5–6, 1986, pp. 607–32.
34 See A. Pizzorno, 'Terrorismo e quadro politico', *Mondo operaio*, XXXI, 1978, 4, pp. 5–18.
35 Ledeen, M., 'Soviet Sponsorship: the Will to Disbelieve', in B. Netanyahu, *Terrorism: How the West Can Win*, New York: Farrar, Strauss, Giroux, 1986, p. 89.
36 Treverton, G.F., *Covert Action. The Limits of Intervention in the Postwar World*, New York: Basic Books, 1987.
37 See Robrieux, P., *La Secte*, Paris: Stock, 1985; Elleinstein, J., *Ils vous trompent, camarades!*, Paris: Belfond, 1981.
38 Aron, R., *Plaidoyer pour l'Europe décadente*, Paris: Laffont 1977, p. 359.
39 It is easy to choose authoritative references in such a wealth of deductions and suppositions; see for instance G. Andreotti, *Diari 1976–1979*, Milano: Rizzoli, 1981, p. 87.
40 See McGwire, M., *Military Objectives in Soviet Foreign Policy*, Washington, D.C.: The Brookings Institution, 1987; Hough, J.F., *The Struggle for the Third World. Soviet Debates and American Options*, Washington, D.C.: The Brookings Institution, 1986.
41 Lacqueur, W., *Reflections on Terrorism* p. 100.
42. *La Repubblica*, 3 November 1988, p. 7.
43. *Il Mattino*, 19 May 1988.
44. Whiteman M., (ed.) *Digest of International Law*, vol. 5, Washington, D. C.: Department of State Publication 1965, pp. 313–14.
45. *La Repubblica*, 20 November 1988, p. 7.
46. Imposimato F., 'Le strategie e i legami tra i terroristi europei e mediorientali', *Speciale Terrorismo Internazionale*, Rome: Adnkronos, 1987, p. 154.
47. Netanyahu B., *Terrorism: How the West Can Win*, New York: Farrar, Strauss, Giroux, 1986, p. 219.
48. See A. F. Panzera, *Attività terroristiche e diritto internazionale*, Naples: Jovene 1978.
49. *The Daily Telegraph*, 16 January 1989, pp. 1, 14.
50. See *Risposta all interrogazione n. 5 – 01110 degli onorevoli Rutelli ed altri*, Bollettino Commissioni, Wednesday 18 June 1989, pp. 41–3.
51. The world of the media is a contradictory reality; some observers have found that the Italian press was featured by many anti-Arab

discriminations. See for instance L. Guazzone (ed.), *Fabbricanti di terrore. Discriminazioni antiarabe nella stampa italiana*, Milano: Sapere 2000 1986. The uprising in Palestine has influenced or justified the relevant change of heart about it.

52. J. La Palombara, *Democracy Italian Style*, New Haven: Yale University Press, 1987, p. 181.
53. S. F. Senigallia, 'The Church and anti-Semitism in Italy', *The New Leader*, 27 June 1988, pp. 5–6.
54 B. Arnett Melchiori, *Terrorism in the Late Victorian Novel*, London: Croom Helm, 1985.
55 See Tribunale di Bari, *Ordinanza di rinvio a giudizio del giudice A. Maritati contro N. Semeraro e altri, e altri atti formali connessi*, Bari: dattiloscritti 1987.
56 This kind of reconstruction has been judged false and factional by many Middle-Eastern governments. The difference between personal responsibilities and institutional responsibilities are enormous; and this is true for all the institutions accused of supporting terrorism.
57 From the quoted hearings of the Head of the Italian police, prefetto Parisi, 6 December 1988, p. 90.
58 They have learned the lesson about 'the extraordinary amount of disruption that a relatively small number of insurgents is able to inflict'; see R. Steel, *Pax Americana: The Cold War Empire and the Practice of Counter-Revolution*, New York: The Viking Press, 1971, p. 293.
59 *Forum*, January 1931.
60 A good description of the old mafia is in F. Sabetti, *Political Authority in a Sicilian Village*, New Brunswick, N. J.: Rutgers University Press, 1984.
61 See the entry 'Mafia', written by G. Mosca, in *The International Encyclopaedia of Social Sciences*, 1930.
62 In these southern neighbourhoods organized crime is filling a vacuum left by the state, providing money, jobs and protection. Even terrorists have sometimes searched the possibility of filling this vacuum; for instance, in Naples, in April 1981, the Red Brigades kidnapped the DC regional assessor for urban planning, exacting as the penalty for his release the housing of earthquake victims and the payment of unemployment compensation to the many jobless citizens in the Neapolitan area. The kidnapping was conducted in collaboration with the Camorra – the predominant criminal organization around Naples.
63 A vivid first-person account in J. Chubb, *Patronage, Power, and Poverty in Southern Italy: A tale of two cities*, Cambridge: Cambridge University Press, 1982; on the same subjects and with an attempt to understand why poverty is connected with organized crime and not with social order, as happens in other parts of the world, see F. Sidoti, *Povertà, devianza, criminalità nell 'Italia meridionale*, Milan: Angeli, 1989.
64 See P. Reuter, 'Eternal Hope: America's International Drug Control Efforts', *The Public Interest*, Spring 1985; and P. Reuter, G. Crawford, J. Cave, *Sealing the Borders*, Santa Monica, Calif: The Rand Corporation, 1988.
65 *The Economist*, 4 June 1988, p. 15.
66 *Newsweek*, 27 February 1989, p. 28.

67   *La Stampa*, 20 January 1989.
68. See A. Touraine, *Production de la société*, Paris: Le Seuil, 1973; M. Crozier and E. Friedberg, *L'Acteur et le Système*, Paris: Le Seuil, 1977.
69. W. Laqueur, 'The Fiction of Intelligence'. *Policy Review*, Summer 1983, p. 90.
70. If I do write, as I hope to, a book about the fictional accounts of factual events, I would remember that the tendency indicated by Laqueur is evident from the beginning of the modern mass-market masterpiece. Balzac notifies the reader that his work 'is neither fiction nor a novel. *All is true*; it is so true that each one can recognize the elements of it surrounding him'.
71. See J. G. Caweli and B. A. Rosenberg, *The Spy Story*, Chicago: University of Chicago Press, 1987.
72. F. Imposimato, in AA. VV., *Perché Moro?*, Roma: Editori Riuniti, 1987, pp. 95–100.

Chapter 6

Do western societies tolerate terrorism?[1]

Noemi Gal-Or

Writing on terrorism, Walter Laqueur, an expert in this field, discusses the traps future scholars might have to avoid: '. . . the historian of the future will be right in pointing to the wide discrepancy between the strong speeches and the weak actions of those who felt threatened [by terrorism]'.[2] He goes on to elaborate on the essence of terrorism and proposes strategies to counter it. These are also supposed to explain the reasons for the discrepancy between the menace felt, so often and so loudly warned against, and the unsatisfying policies applied to counter it.

Another author has also pointed at 'the disparate relationship between the actual threat of terrorism and [the fact that] responses to it are pivoted on an intermediary factor of *perceived threat*.' Jenny Hocking thus argues rightly that: 'The depiction of terrorism as a threat to the state introduces an immediate discrepancy between the actual impact of terrorism and the perceived threat presented by it. This in turn interrelates with the preventive measures taken against terrorism.'[3]

A similar observation concerning the continuity of terrorism (and the increasing application of 'terrorism' to a variety of political behaviours) in western society, together with the alarm still raised, leads us, however, to pose a somewhat different question. While traditonally assumed and agreed by many scholars that the threat of terrorism (real or perceived, against the state or the person and so on and so forth)[4] cannot be tolerated by liberal democracies and these are only structurally restricted in effectively countering the challenge, we dare suggest a different explanation. Consequently, it is not the anti-terrorist strategies applied by western liberal-democratic governments that concern us. Rather, it is the other side of the coin which is intriguing, indeed, provoking: are the western liberal democracies of the mid- to late-twentieth century terrorism-tolerating systems?

Further variations may be derived from this key question. For instance, does there prevail a certain practical (though probably not theoretical) level of tolerance of terrorism which is tenable, even necessary and system-conditioned? If so, is it possible to discern a certain golden path of tolerance? Must it be that tolerance always means agreement, consent and approval of terrorism whereas intolerance axiomatically equals the pure and noble moralistic stand? Or, translated into a less normative dimension, referring to the implementation of anti-terrorist policies: does tolerating terrorism always mean being more liberal and conscious of human rights while not tolerating necessarily amounts to oppression, coercion and disregard of these rights?

If these premises are not exhaustive and mutually exclusive, then there should be a third way of evaluating liberal-democratic governments' response to terrorism and western society's reaction to it. Namely, the outcomes of western societies' encounter with the phenomenon of modern terrorism does not necessarily and only imply a failure of the strategy applied. Although it seems obvious to say so, the explanation may well be the unwillingness, lack of motivation and or interest to do more, probably based on practical and pragmatic considerations. This does not amount to any moral condemnation whatsoever. The discussion here is not whether intransigence and applying all the resources available against terrorism is morally good or bad. Rather it is the functionality of terrorism and anti-terrorism[5] that is significant: terrorism as contributing to the social and political order in the target system; terrorism as a means to regulate various political or social strains and contraints; terrorism as a welcome political scape-goat in liberal-democratic societies and polities. In other words, terrorism is not *always* and *deterministically* even a perceived threat and not *necessarily* a destabilizing factor.

A dialectical process seems to dictate the policy of democratic societies towards terrorism. As long as terrorism is no more than a nuisance, a democracy will rightly resist any attempt to curtail its traditional freedoms. Once terrorism becomes more than a nuisance, once the normal functioning of society is affected, there will be overwhelming pressure on the government to defeat the threat by all available means.[6]

Laqueur is certainly correct to point out the importance of the degree of terrorism. In fact, he goes on further to discuss the relevance of various kinds of terrorism as affecting governmental reaction. These include basically two significant versions, in addition to domestic terrorism: state-sponsored terrorism and international terrorism (sometimes overlapping). Hence, governments, depending upon the menace felt (inextricably related to the notion of legitimacy), might at times be reserved and self-contained in their response, while on other occasions they would opt for resoluteness and may even be driven to over-react.

We suggest adding another dimension to this argument, the time dimension that coincides with experience gained from the encounter with terrorism. Dealing with western liberal democracies, it has become evident that after the first shock of being challenged by terrorism in the mid- to late-1960s, and by natural way of trial and error, governments as well as societies have learned both to respond to this new phenomenon as well as live with it. Furthermore, it is important to add that governments and elements in society have learned to *exploit* terrorism directed against them, to manipulate terrorism in their favour. This has depended undoubtedly, on the kind of terrorism encountered. Indeed, the combination of experience-with-terrorism and nature-of-terrorism has resulted in a rather flexible threshold of tolerance of terrorism.

Tolerating terrorism may vary by degree. After all, tolerance is dynamic and stretches from tacit consent through connivance, and active consent as far as support and co-operation. *The Encyclopedia of the Social Sciences* emphasizes the relativity of this property very clearly:

> ... it appears to them [people condemning or deploring in- tolerance in others] bad in some cases and good in other cases; bad when it is intolerance of the good and good when it is intolerance of the bad. Intolerance in the abstract has lost caste, but abstract intolerance happens to be of no social significance. And it is generally agreed that in the concrete a point is invariably reached beyond which tolerance ceases to be a virtue. In other words, contemporary conditions of life enforce a practical kind of toleration and leave the intolerant spirit largely untouched.[7]

In other words, there is room for a variety of expressions for tolerance, ranging on a continuum from absolute intolerance to active tolerance in the form of support and co-operation. Yet, since tolerance is extremely subjective, it will unfold differently even within politically similar societies.

The origin of this book is an attempt to understand tolerance of terrorism in principle, and the varying degrees of tolerance of terrorism within five western liberal democracies: Spain, Belgium, the Federal Republic of Germany, Italy and Middle-Eastern Israel. Each of the contributors to this collection has addressed the same topic and was guided by the same research questions. The approaches diverged significantly, however. First comes the personal aptitude and background of the author: Hans-Joseph Horchem was responsible, in the Federal Republic of Germany, for anti-terrorist policy and its implementation. Horchem thus maintains a different approach from Peter Waldemann the sociologist, Francesco Sidoti who is also an historian or Simon Peterman and Noemi Gal-Or, the political scientists. Essentially a normative notion, what is regarded as highly tolerant in one country and by one author, may consequently be considered as intolerant by another. The goal of this project is, however, not to standardize the case studies, which would have violated the authenticity of the research, but to reveal the common denominators that prevail despite evident and typical differences.

More significant, however, is that despite the fact that all the countries are liberal democracies, these regimes are quite distinct from each other. Spain represents a very recent and young democracy, which is of particular importance when compared to the rest of the countries studied here. All of the European states reviewed are present members of the European Community, which testifies for the stability governing their relationships, directed at augmenting harmony and integration. Except for the Federal Republic of Germany's former specific foreign-political concerns with regard to the (now past) German Democratic Republic and its location on the (old) border between east and west, it is Israel – contrary to the other case studies – that is almost completely encircled by enemy states. Moreover, each of the countries reviewed provides for its specific mixture of kinds of terrorism. Belgium is plagued mainly by a 'unidimensional' type of terrorism, namely revolutionary-ideological, while Italy has had to cope with the challenge of various kinds of domestic terrorism, international terrorism – both European and Middle-Eastern – state-sponsored terrorism and narco-terrorism.

Is it then possible to draw any kind of general conclusions as to the tolerance of terrorism in the west? Can we expect to be able to discern any patterns common to those distinct examples?

We are convinced that despite variations and since all five case studies reported belong to basically the same political-ideological regime, some comparisons are not only possible, they are even mandatory. It is a matter of fact that there is a prevailing unanimity of ideas that lie at the basis of liberal democracy: delegitimization of non-governmental and non-political violence, along with delegitimization of violence in matters of domestic politics which include the absolute denunciation of terrorism in this normative category (clearly, governmental violence has also its moral and ideological limits here).[8] This is an elementary common denominator of all the liberal democracies discussed here by definition of their democratic virtue. It is therefore the standard against which the effective tolerance of terrorism within the five states should be measured.[9]

Two major questions guide our comparison: (a) What kind of attitudes have the given *polities* developed towards terrorism and terrorists? (b) What sort of attitude have the given *societies* developed towards terrorism and terrorists? By juxtaposing the governmental attitudes among themselves and against the attitudes of the public, we hope to reach some general conclusions as to the tolerance of terrorism in western liberal democracies.

GOVERNMENTAL ATTITUDES TO TERRORISM AND TERRORISTS

An ideal democratic government would be one whose actions were *always* in perfect correspondence with the preferences of *all* its citizens. Such complete responsiveness in government has never existed and may never be achieved, but it can serve as an ideal to which democratic regimes should aspire. It can also be regarded as the end of a scale on which the degree of democratic responsiveness of different regimes may be measured. . . . These democratic regimes ['polyarchies'] are characterized not by perfect responsiveness but by a high degree of it: their actions have been in *relatively close* correspondence with the wishes of *relatively many* of their citizens for a *long period of time*.[10]

Paraphrasing this quote from Lijphart's *Democracies* it is evidently possible to replace 'preferences' and 'wishes' of the citizens with 'values' of society. Hence, government may react in different ways to terrorism, that is, to the threatening of the preferences of the citizens: either to the threat to law and order (including personal security) and/or to the value of rejecting violence in public political life.

Governments will endorse an intransigent attitude against terrorism and against terrorists.

Terrorism is basically applied in order to threaten a certain regime, to undermine its legitimacy and alienate the public from the government through the instigation of instability resulting from fear.[11] While this is the premise of the terrorist strategy, the achievement of these objectives depend to a large extent on the specific circumstance in which terrorism is being applied. In other words, depending upon various conditions, terrorists have to allow more or less time for the strategy to become effective. Effectiveness of terrorism is first and foremost measured by the fear inspired in the target – population and government alike. Terrorism will be interpreted as such by governments only when the threat is perceived to be real, direct and urgent.

There are specific and alternative kinds of conditions under which a government becomes especially vulnerable to such threatening pressure:

(a)   Governments are caught by surprise; they are not ready for the challenge of terrorism;

(b)   The terrorists enjoy widespread support or approval within a significant sector of the population, and the approval is persistent over a long period of time; or,

(c)   Support of the cause of terrorism and often the method itself relates to fundamental and central issues within the targeted system.

Given these basic conditions, the declared and resolute anti-terrorism and anti-terrorist disposition may develop at two alternative points of time:

(a)   Anti-terrorism as a first immediate reaction to the terrorist struggle at its initial stages;

(b)   Anti-terrorism as outcome of a failure to overcome terrorism by other means, and the consequent strengthening of terrorism.

Reviewing the case studies analysed earlier, the first alternative seems more typical to the experience of the given democracies than the second one.

The German experience with the Red Army Faction (RAF) points to a combination of the unpreparedness of the government and surprise. The German government responded in a way which was as close as possible to the imperatives of the 'ideal' rejection of violence in liberal democracies' political game. German revolutionary-ideological, left-wing terrorism also impinged on the very sensitive issue of the viability of the renewed German democracy, which was dependent upon the purity of the system with regard to its genuinely democratically oriented representatives: 'In many newspaper articles the behaviour of the sympathizers was explained by comparison to the Gestapo era, during which citizens gave refuge to resistance fighters fleeing from the police pursuing them.' (see p. 37.)

In his chapter, Horchem indirectly alludes to the firmness of the German government's response to domestic terrorism. This stand has been reflected in the terrorist propaganda too. While overdoing their blame for the government for the illegality of its methods, terrorists have nevertheless propagated a message not welcomed by the authorities: 'The main accusation of the publications [of the terrorists] in question was that conservative forces were using the fight against terrorism to set up a "police surveillance state" in the Federal Republic.'[12] Notwithstanding the legitimacy of the German anti-terrorism measures, it evidently illustrates that terrorism was absolutely rejected. (See pp. 46 and 47.)

The Israeli anti-terrorist position (described in chapter 3) has been consistently pursued as far back as the creation of the state of Israel. Its rejection of terrorism must be understood in two contexts. The first, more evident context is that of Palestinian terrorism. This is the case where terrorism enjoys widespread approval and support among a relatively extensive but deeply hostile national group within the population and, the endorsement of terrorism is persistent over a very long period of time.

In the Israeli case, this kind of terrorism has been indeed understood in terms of an existential threat right from the beginning. Hence, there existed no contradiction between the normative imperative of opposing terrorism as an evil threatening democracy and the specific view of Palestinian terrorism as an evil threatening Jewish-Israeli national survival. Intransigence was the ultimate policy to be adopted. This approach has also prevailed for a long time in respect to Jewish-Israeli terrorism. Though minor in terms of public legitimacy and marginal in its appearances, this kind of terrorism, coinciding with the early years of the establishment of the state of Israel, put in question the viability of the system and its young regime. Here too, the circumstances and the novelty of the phenomenon combined to result in a terrorism-intolerant governmental response. As a matter of fact, this and not Palestinian terrorism was the reason to initiate the first Anti-Terrorism Decree of 1948.

Basque terrorism in Spain definitely belongs to the category of extensive and persistent support within a population overwhelmingly opposed to the central government. As a matter of fact, the Spanish democratic government has found itself carrying over an intransigent attitude towards Basque terrorism which originated in the dictatorial regime of General Franco. Basque terrorism not only enjoyed popular approval, it has been related also to most central issues in Spanish politics. While the power of the centre was contested during the Franco regime, the integration of the Spanish multi-ethnic state and the viability of the young and struggling-for-life democracy were at stake. Thus, right from its inception, the Spanish democratic government was forced to deal with an already long-standing terrorist situation, and the only suitable response to that challenge has been absolute intolerance of terrorism. According to Peter Waldemann (chapter 1): 'Only a clear breach with the Francoist government system by the new democratic leadership elite could have prevented this transference effect. As we know, such a breach has not taken place – neither generally nor with regard to the attitude of the central authorities towards the Basque minority . . . The Spanish security forces continued to use a strong hand at demonstrations in the region of Cantabria' (p. 6).

It is rather easy and even more fortunate to have had an anti-terrorist position from the very start of the terrorist problem. Once a government has empirically proved its firmness against terrorism, it has established its credibility and can in the future capitalize on the confidence vested in it by means of anti-terrorist rhetoric only. In other words, terrorism in certain circumstances runs the risk of exhausting itself and losing the battle to alienate people and government. Even in Israel, Palestinians tired of the political limits to terrorism, burst out into far more effective civil disobedience and revolt struggle. Once successfully past this threshold, however, the authorities can contend with verbal anti-terrorism while switching over to quite different empirical and practical means of countering terrorism (which will be the topic of the next section). There is still left, however, the second, somewhat exceptional type of governmental intolerance to terrorism, illustrated by the Italian case.

Francesco Sidoti (chapter 5) says: 'The Italian terroristic events are confused with the darkest events of the recent Italian political life, from Mafia crimes to covert operations ruled by local and foreign secret services.'(p. 105.) Italian terrorism, as described here, appears to be 'independent' in the sense that it does not fulfil the usual theoretical conditions of terrorism. Pointing at the too narrow overlapping of 'private/individual' political terrorism and illegal use or abuse of power by the covert violence of public and governmental bodies, Sidoti makes it quite clear that Italian authorities have switched over to an intransigent struggle against terrorism only after having failed to control it otherwise.

To be sure, those counter-terrorist efforts, characterized by the negation of the terrorist cause and terrorism as a method relate notably to the revolutionary-ideological type of terrorism in Italy, i.e. the Red Brigades and the pseudo-masonic and right-wing Lodge P2 terrorism. Other sources of terrorism have been either endured as long as they were controllable by means of 'buying' relative law and order and stability (i.e., South-Tyrol), or meticulously and discriminately manipulated by the central authorities (giving rise to allegations of CIA-inspired terrorism, the mafia, drug-trafficking and Middle-Eastern terrorism). The ruling authorities were shaken out of their indifference only when terrorism started to exceed the tolerable limits and began to undermine their reputation. Also, anti-Red Brigades efforts were undertaken only after the failure of the Italian political establishment, namely the political parties, to 'juggle' with the imprisoned terrorists – to exploit the terrorists and the information they were believed to possess as electoral assets in the inter-party competition. Indeed, once the anti-terrorist legislation of 1979–80 had been launched, and later the rehabilitation programme introduced, revolutionary-ideological terrorism was successfully reduced.

The political system is acquiescent of terrorism and does not develop an anti-terrorist disposition in principle.

Applying the negative rather than the affirmative is the appropriate semantics to describe this category of terrorism-oriented attitude. We do not maintain here that authorities willingly or deliberately support terrorism and co-operate with terrorists, rather, we point to the fact that, under certain circumstances, governments, the legislature or the judicial apparatus might remain indifferent, perhaps tolerant of terrorism.

This sort of attitude can develop only under conditions where terrorism does not present a perceived direct threat to central interests or values. Such weakness of terrorism can usually be attributed to one major reason (with two variations): either the terrorists do not enjoy sufficient popular support right from the start, or the terrorists are not convincing enough in their claim and therefore have no potential in mobilizing and crystallizing any significant popular support in the future. Consequently, the acts of terrorism, the violent assaults, are understood as accessories to either those weak dissident political or social groups or organizations, or to actors who are less relevant to domestic politics. It is expected that terrorism, the method, will expire from itself, together with the dissolution of its carriers. In addition, it has anyway become a matter of general acceptance, that terrorism forms an integral part of modern political life.

Like in other matters of politics, in this context too, pragmatism and realism rather than moralism are guiding the political decision-makers. Consequently, tolerance of terrorism derives from the recognition that there are modern socio-political issues which carry, by definition a predisposition for terrorism. This would be the case in particular, of national-separatist concerns, racism and anti-semitism, and the like. The crucial reason for tolerance is the absence of an imminent and direct threat to the integrity and stability of the regime.

Reviewing our western European case studies reveals Belgium as a typical example. Middle-Eastern terrorism and anti-Jewish terrorism resulted in fewer repercussions on the Belgian official counter-terrorist stance than did the ideological-revolutionary type. This does, however, fit in with the overall Belgian reaction which, is described by Petermann (chapter 4) as being rather reserved and unaffected (p. 95). Thus, also, the Spanish experience with isolated Middle-Eastern terrorist assaults seems not to have aroused any particular concerns and trouble. Basque terrorists still overwhelmingly dominate Spanish attention; others are less significant. Nor has Germany been alarmed by right-wing terrorism the way it has been shaken by left-wing terrorists as far as inducing the impression of a country under emergency. The arrest of the leaders of the neo-Nazi organizations has seemed to cut the ground from under any future prospects of mobilization. Horchem is therefore confident that 'Terrorism of the right does not represent a real threat for the time being.'(See p. 56.)

Authorities' tolerance of terrorism

The indifferent attitude, the one logically between the extremes of absolute negation of terrorism and some level of tolerance, is rare. In fact, the conflict of moralist–ideological versus empirical and pragmatist requirements is too sharp to allow for compromise. The predicaments are fundamental: terrorism can be either good or evil. Since the idea of liberal democracy is based on peaceful persuasion into agreement, violence is clearly an abrogation of this principle, and so is terrorism. Indifference towards terrorism, at least theoretically, means in moral terms moving away from the rejection towards the collaborative-tolerating end of the continuum. Omission still bears responsibility for wrong-doing. Consequently, regulating the defined-wrong so as to avoid trying to eradicate it would morally be unsustainable in a democracy. Noam Chomsky is extremely outspoken is this respect. His example is obviously taken from the American political experience, which he characterizes as governed by a terrorist culture. Though different, even contrary to our discourse, it nevertheless holds some grains of relevance to our context too:

> the state is relatively limited, by comparative standards, in the capacity to control its population by force, and must therefore rely more heavily on the more subtle devices of imagination and doctrine. The culture of terrorism that has grown in our midst is a structure of considerable power, with an impressive arsenal of devices to protect itself from the threat of understanding and with a powerful base in the institutions that dominate every facet of social life – the economy and political institutions, the intellectual culture and much of the popular culture as well.[13]

Indeed, in practice liberal democracy constantly violates its own premises. Nevertheless, it can and does survive by coming close to its ideal even if not necessarily fully accomplishing it. Altering the stance towards values to enable smooth compromise with reality-dictated constraints is on the daily agenda of the liberal democracies. This holds true also in respect to violence and, in the present context, to terrorism, a particular branch of politically motivated violence. By denouncing the signs of partial consent and regulated violence, scholars, journalists and jurists contribute to the improvement and perfecting of democracy, thus performing the gate-keeper's role. These are the imperative and indispensable dynamics which guarantee survival of liberal democracy.

Consequently, politicians who declare and announce their steadfast anti-terrorist commitment are not misleading their audience. They restate and reaffirm the values of liberal democracy, they recall attention to one of the basic values, hence to the model of liberal democracy. In practice, however, they will too often look for avenues to evade the impossibilities or difficulties resulting from confronting terrorism by the moral imperatives. Indeed, under certain conditions, co-operating with terrorism could prove to be the lesser among evils in order to rid oneself of a certain type of terrorism; this could be a way to minimize the democracy-corrupting effect of terrorism. The boundary between this apparently legitimate tolerance of terrorism and the illegitimate comprehension of terrorism is very narrow. Crossing from one side to the other could be interpreted as switching from strengthening to undermining the democratic regime.

Ruling authorities will prove tolerant to terrorism – from supporting exchange deals with terrorists to non-prosecution of terrorists, to the selfish exploitation of terrorism which amounts to co-operation. The choice of the appropriate policy will depend upon the expected goal. The policies are ordered here according to their degree of compliance with liberal-democratic perceptions concerning the legitimacy of the use of violence:

Control over sources of terrorism and related factors

Often governments will comply with some aspects of terrorism as a weapon in their anti-terrorist campaign. Governments might pragmatically choose to solve the short-term problem caused by terrorism rather than confront the remote aim of eradicating terrorism as such.

Italy opted for 'buying' order and social and political tranquillity in South-Tyrol by preferential economic investment. Satisfying people's demand and accommodating them by favouring them over others has proved cheaper to democracy when measured against the cost of selling out some democratic values in order to secure others.

Also, by co-operating with certain terrorist elements, governments have often attempted to isolate others. The heterogeneity of the terrorist scene will lead the authorities responsible for law and order to select between imminent terrorist threats and less menacing ones. As the German and Italian cases have proved in respect to Middle-Eastern terrorism, giving a *laissez passer* to Palestinian terrorists and reaching understanding with these foreign terrorists in exchange for abolishing their ties with domestic terrorists was an efficient tool in curbing the more threatening and intensive local terrorism, though at the ethical price of being selfish rather than moral.[14]

This kind of pragmatism can be traced, to a limited extent, in the change in Israel's anti-terrorism policy which took place in the late 1970s. Letting itself be dragged into exchange-deals with Palestinian terrorists seemed at that time viable, particularly after having succeeded in reducing the level of domestic terrorism to the minimum possible. Turning a blind eye to Jewish terrorism by refraining from prosecuting its most violent component – the Jewish Underground organization – has to some degree had to do with trying not to 'awake the lions from their rest'. Underreaction here, that is, non-exposure and non-prosecution for as long as possible, was partially aimed at choking Jewish terrorist enthusiasm.

Terrorism exploited as a means to win in domestic political rivalries

The toleration, even co-operation and coming to terms with certain terrorist groups in a kind of gentlemen's agreement has been described above. This section reveals the rather cynical attitude adopted by certain governmental and other related public authorities with regard to individual terrorists. Terrorism as a political method is irrelevant in this context. The identity of the terrorists and the impact of their deeds is the crucial factor here.

As has been pointed out in the Israeli case study, connivance and shortcomings – both in the uncovering of the Jewish Underground and in the judicial procedure and its aftermath – have been deeply embedded in political interests. Understood as no serious challenge to democracy itself (albeit a threat to state, since the attempt at Temple Mount, could have potentially entailed a *Jihad*, i.e. all-state Muslim holy war against Israel), and even supportive in its ideological premise, this terrorism was abused and exploited to enhance electoral and power-political assets. The consistent emphasis on the need to distinguish the terrorists from terrorism – the doers from their deeds – further manifests the politicization of the anti-terrorist disposition.

A similar process, also including the executive, the legislature and, to some extent, the judiciary holds for Italy. This is portrayed by Sidoti (chapter 5), notably in the case of the anti-communist manipulation of terrorism by the Italian political parties. Such allegations have been made against the German authorities as well. Refuted by Horchem (chapter 2), the theory of 'state's conspiracy', which accused the security services of instigating terrorism of the left so as to fortify state surveillance and power, evoked some repercussions at the time.[15]

Terrorism exploited as a means in the relations between the centre and other factors in society and/or outside the country

Terrorism as a cheap way either to wage low-intensity war or to blackmail governments in diplomatic interaction has become known as state-sponsored terrorism. The present category of reasons for tolerating terrorism by liberal-democratic governments differs from state-sponsored terrorism by the fact that terrorism is not embedded in its formal policy or strategy. Rather, terrorism has occurred independently, ending up with governments or other bodies within the ruling authorities profiting from the opportunity to 'jump on the bandwagon'.

The chapter dealing with the Israeli experience clearly demonstrates how Jewish-Israeli terrorism has been perceived as an effective signal to Palestinian terrorists. Endorsing the justness of the cause of Jewish terrorism means by the same token delegitimizing anti-Israeli terrorism. In other words, Jewish terrorism has become a factor in the relations of Israeli authorities with the Palestinians.

The Italian case seems much more complex. The allegations about foreign involvement (CIA interference) in Italian politics are refuted by Sidoti. Other connections do none the less exist. Italy is worried that economic relations in the Middle East would be damaged if Middle-Eastern terrorism was severely prosecuted. It also fears the threat to Italy's stability from expansionist Islamic fundamentalism. The ultimate response is therefore to accommodate the more moderate and economically important partner even at the price of giving in to terrorism, even by concluding deals with Palestinian terrorists (p. 128). In fact, there prevails unanimity all through the

Italian establishment with regard to Palestinian terrorism: support of the PLO and its cause without referring to terrorism, and criticism of Israel by the Pope, the media, bureaucracy, trade unions, government and communist opposition. More active involvement is revealed with regard to the manipulation of terrorism, in particular of right-wing terrorism, to serve the interests of the mafia. Yet the mafia is not unique in this context: 'These organizations [belonging to the Mafia] have relations with terrorist groups, high level politicians, equivocal businessmen who work in laundering and recycling dirty money. The head of the Italian police stated: "In such an entangled situation terrorist acts of great emotional impact are committed, actions which have the immediate consequence of inducing the judges, the police, the anti-mafia Commissioner, the intelligence services to deviate every investigative effort to other fields, conceding in this way a large relief to organized crime."' (See p. 133.)

In this case, the intricate web of political and economic factors and actors suggests the possibility that political-ideological terrorism becomes exploited as a 'mercenary' for pragmatic politico-economic purposes. The existence of organized crime manipulating the ruling authorities and politicizing the economy by terrorist methods poses the question whether this can be still considered as 'terrorism', or whether conditioning terrorism as a cover, belongs already to a different category of violence.

Reviewing the three different ways western liberal-democratic authorities respond to terrorism – intransigent intolerance, almost indifferent acquiescence, and approving and supporting tolerance – reveals that in real politics, to be distinguished from the ideological vocation, such regimes are indeed split and divided in their attitude to terrorism.

Though unanimous about the moral values, they are by no means consistent in their policy, either concerning terrorism as a phenomenon and a policy tool, or concerning the terrorist organizations themselves as actors and political factors. A state's pragmatic disposition towards the phenomenon of terrorism cannot be divorced from its attitude to the terrorist. Indeed, the claim that 'one man's terrorist is another man's freedom fighter' is not necessarily true when dealing with liberal democracies. In fact, the conflict between moral imperatives and practical politics invalidates this correlation and renders it rather irrelevant.

Hence, to the question 'what can democracies do when wishing to counter terrorism?', the answer should be: do not rely primarily on the moral common denominator and, therefore, do not take co-operation for granted. Rather, governments should look for pragmatic common interest, and the answer will lie there. When interests overlap or are compatible, one or more of the following instrumental categories will apply:

Co-operating through supporting terrorism and terrorists in order to eradicate them;
Co-operating through support of terrorism and terrorists in order to benefit from and exploit it/them;
Co-operating through countering terrorism and terrorists in order to eradicate them.

The fear of terrorism, or intimidation inspired by terrorism does not derive from terrorism as a special method of behaviour. The effect of terrorism cannot be separated from its cause and its perpetrators. In other words, terror felt and sensed is not abstract. Terrorization depends on the specific terrorists who invoke the reaction of the authorities. Though democratic governments apparently respond to the threat of the phenomenon, they do in fact react to the specific perpetrator of the threat. Fearing the violence of terrorism is no different from fearing armed robbery or rape. Fearing terrorism in a particular political context is much more plausible and real. Consequently, denouncing all 'terrorism' and under all circumstances, is not always reckoned to be functional in countering it. After all, terrorism in practice (not in theory) is not necessarily and not always a threat to the specific democratic regime of the state where it happens to be perpetrated. This explains the tolerance of terrorism and even co-operation with terrorists by liberal-democratic governments.

SOCIETY'S ATTITUDE TOWARDS TERRORISM AND TERRORISTS

As in other matters, a feedback cycle operates between government and public administration and society with regard to the attitude to terrorism.[16] The authorities response to terrorism affects society's level of tolerance to terrorism and the terrorists, and vice versa. Input from various elements of the public influence the stand adopted by the ruling institutions towards the same phenomenon and actors. This is not to say that the positions taken share the same direction or are consensual. All too often society is split about terrorism (both in respect of the instrumentality of terrorism as a pragmatic means of achieving goals and the terrorist claim and cause), so that part of the public agrees with the official policy, but other elements, on the contrary, object and dissent. Hence, depending upon the circumstances, governmental policy might result in the opposite feedback from the population. Overreaction might alienate, while underreaction might enrage those feeling exposed to the danger. Consequently, it is incorrect to refer to a unified attitude of society towards terrorism, even if the ideological premise of the liberal-democratic society presumes a categorical rejection.

There comes first, obviously, the legal option. Legislation as a procedure reflects, in liberal democracy, the extent to which society is ready to carry the burden of terrorism, and what price it is willing to pay. Here again it becomes obvious that the degree of threat felt is the real measure applied to deciding upon the legal tools available. Thus society adapts itself to the specific pertinent characteristics of terrorism.

In the Federal Republic of Germany stiffening the laws entailed a massive backlash from particular social sectors. Lawyers themselves switched over to the 'terrorist environment' extending its political influence as the 'legal arm' of the terrorists (pp. 37 and 45). These lawyers were not content with strictly legal support, but engaged in a public campaign for the protection of the human and civil rights of the terrorists (p. 41). Horchem's case study conveys the impression that such legal assistance exceeded the limits of democratic equity and came closer to support of terrorism itself. This agitation even crossed national boundaries to include the 'legal periphery' from sympathizing jurists in other European countries. In other words, the interaction of the government and public in the German case resulted in a partial divorce between legal authorities and legal practitioners.

A similar counter-reaction has been visible in the Basque case as well. Waldemann devotes an extensive discussion to describing the Gestoras por Amnistia which aim to improve the prison conditions of the imprisoned Etarras, and even more, to create favourable conditions to enable them to pursue political activities within the prison walls. Gestoras have been active on both local/regional and national/international levels and have definitely supported the ETA in its struggle and the terrorists as individuals.

Help from the legal establishment also characterizes the Israeli 'pro-terrorist' scene. Indeed, Palestinian terrorists have had to contend in this field with the exhaustion of standard available means. Jewish terrorists however, have enjoyed support which has extended and evolved into efforts to modify or add to existing legislation so as to tailor it to their special needs. Pardon and amnesty have been frequently introduced on the legislative agenda when referring to Jewish terrorism, whereas when the promotion of capital punishment has recurred, it was always with regard to Palestinian terrorists.

The Italian case study does not elaborate on the legislative aspect of tolerating terrorism beyond mentioning the 'stick and carrot' policy (comprising of a combination of anti-terrorist legislation and a rehabilitation programme). The Belgian case study testifies to indifference, or at least strong belief and trust on behalf of society in the authorities' ability to manage the situation.

There are other sources of support besides the legislative and legal fields in which tolerance of terrorism finds expression. In fact, the legal discourse has been only one avenue among many extensively used by the intelligentsia. Revolutionary-ideological terrorism in West Germany has overwhelmingly appealed to the 'thinker' elitist sector of society. Despite being the pretentious avant-garde of the working class, this supposed benefactor never mobilized to support them. Intellectuals and the New Left continued to lead as 'guardians' of the terrorists' rights after the expiration of the short and initial mythicized and romanticized public excitement unleashed by the early assaults.

Basically, support has come from an elitist group, which explains its failure in filtering down to the vast majority of ordinary people. Its rhetoric (the distinct jargon) has been too sophisticated for it to be understood by the non-academic public. The contents have not been the promotion of the very ambiguous and vague ideology of the terrorists, but rather the incrimination of the authorities for suppression of freedom and Nazism. Even the attempt to evoke compassion for the allegedly mishandled terrorist prisoners has failed to mobilize public opinion, since both language and interests were not shared by the public at large. Writers, journalists, philosophers and others have been intensively involved in this campaign (for example Heinrich Böll or Jean-Paul Sartre). Their influence in matters of terrorism though, was limited to a very restricted circle on top of the socio-economic ladder. This isolation of the thinking elite explains perhaps why Germany has succeeded in providing the model for co-operation between media and authorities as best demonstrated in the Schleyer case. Indeed, the role of the intelligentsia in either controlling and containing or promoting political violence, is a complex phenomenon definitely deserving a separate study.

Since terrorism in Italy has been so multifaceted and too often related to public scandals, support from private sectors has not been as noticeable as in Germany. The rhetoric campaign has been limited mainly to manifestos and communiqués circulated by the terrorists, reproduced in the newspapers and discussed by isolated professors in particular universities. Even in the case of nationalist South-Tyrolian terrorism, the support of the public has been rather limited. On the other hand, Italians have occasionally organized in rallies, usually for funerals of distinguished victims of terrorism, to demonstrate against terrorism and the terrorists.

The Basque case study clearly provides an example for continuing widespread popular endorsement of the terrorist cause (and in the past also of the terrorist method). The disenfranchised lower middle class is the main bastion of support, though even here democracy has attenuated the enthusiasm. While in the past the whole social and cultural life of the Basque community was mobilized in support of terrorism (as a manifestation of the struggle for self-determination), the diminishing support and its concentration, in particular among the unemployed youth, has created new channels for expression such as the 'radical Basque rock'. A variety of other means, from supporting youth organizations to hunger strikes, etc., are among the accepted tactics of expressing identification with the terrorists.

This has also been the case in respect to Jewish-Israeli terrorism and, obviously to a much more restricted extent, also regarding Palestinian terrorism. Rhetoric manipulation is an outstanding element in the support of the Jewish terrorists and it is accompanied, for additional impact, with religious linguistic flavour. To be sure, populism is a strong source of terrorist support in Israeli society, where such interest groups as the settlers are intimately entwined with figures from the various public sectors: jurisdiction, legislation, religious authority and government. Hunger strikes, public opinion polls, rallies, demonstrations and petitions are among other means, visible expressions not merely of tolerance, but also of support.

As Petermann notes, Belgian terrorism has been 'unbacked' terrorism. The minimalistic outspokenness in favour of Belgian terrorists should, however, reflect indifference more than strict rejection.

The most important insight to be gained from the above comparison refers to the relativism of terrorism within liberal-democratic society. Terrorism is not necessarily and always perceived as the ultimate evil endangering the survival of the regime. While democratic governments have indeed abused the notion of terrorism (the purpose of this being a subject for a separate essay), it is not true that their audience has always fallen prey to it.

CONCLUSION

The Italian and Israeli case studies reflect the fusion and confusion, the blurring of boundaries between the private and the public sectors. Rather than rising from some basic tolerance of terrorism, this is the outcome of political interests, and it is of secondary significance whether these interests are conditioned by socio-economic or nationalistic considerations. It seems, therefore, that interest and power politics are also more important in the context of terrorism. Despite the heavy value-loading of this notion, pragmatism overshadows ideological or thematic concerns however significant these might be.

Applying the traditional classification of types of terrorism might be useful in generalizing and drawing the conclusion from the above case study comparison.

Revolutionary-ideological terrorism invites tolerance of terrorism and terrorists in very particular social sectors, clearly discernible in socio-economic and cultural patterns. The more educated and the better-off, far more than those on the lower echelons of status, have tended to tolerate, indeed to support terrorism. The intellectual's role in the support of German RAF terrorism and the Italian Red Brigades as well as Lodge P2 support from the mighty politico-economic sector, and the very marginal justification by intellectuals of terrorism in Belgium represent a pool of support, though limited in scope. In fact, revolutionary-ideological terrorism does not enjoy popular support. Nevertheless, while the actual impact of the elitist sector on public opinion has been rather modest, it has been more significant in places where the political decisions concerning terrorism are made. In other words, the quality of the carriers of support is no less important than the quantity of those tolerating it. This reflects the fact that liberal-democratic society is capable of tolerating terrorism and in fact does so without entailing severe damage.

Separatist-nationalist terrorism recruits its support from the defined ethnic sectors it claims to be representing. Ethnic solidarity is certainly stronger than class solidarity.[17] This means that tolerance of terrorism all too often succeeds in cutting across socio-economic barriers. Some limitations are nevertheless visible: in the Basque region, the upper class comprising of wealthy industrialists objects to terrorism which interrupts good business. In Israel, support and tolerance depend on one's political conviction. In general, tolerance of nationalistic motivated terrorism in Spain and Israel has been much more popular in numerical terms.

Indeed, separatist-nationalist terrorism has been more disruptive to the liberal-democratic regime than its revolutionary-ideological counterpart. Spain in its transition to democracy realized that. Spanish, including Basque, concerns that terrorism might sabotage the process of democratization have helped not only to expand denunciation of terrorism but also to curb support for ETA. On the other hand, in Israel, Palestinian terrorism never seemed to endanger democracy (to be distinguished from security). Jewish terrorism (and other factors as well) could capitalize on this precedent-setting terrorist experience. Indeed, it is precisely because of the illusive feeling of 'democratic immunity' that it has succeeded in enlisting even more than simple tolerance.

While terrorism might be the trigger, the reason for the attitude taken to terrorism is too often embedded in the *cause* of terrorism, and not in the anti-democratic method of behaviour itself. Moreover, another rather trivial explanation for the variation in the attitude towards terrorism lies in the terrorist tactics themselves. The RAF's targets were rather selective and did not include the intelligentsia elitist supporters. This holds also for Italy and the Jewish-Israeli cases. Spain witnessed a change in the character of ETA terrorism, which started and continued for a long period as discriminate. Later, when challenged with democratization it switched to indiscriminate targeting, which resulted in reduced support. In Belgium, terrorism has broken all rules of the game and is characterized by a complete absence of logic which has resulted in the alienation of the majority of the population.

The extent and scope of tolerance for terrorism is certainly affected by the degree of fear and terror inspired within the afflicted population. This varies from country to country. While supportable on moral grounds, absolute negation of terrorism has failed to be translated as a constant variable either into governmental policy or social reality. When all is said and done, it is in the end the right dose of flexible tolerance which will safeguard the liberal-democratic balance between the rights of the individual and the security of the whole community.

NOTES

1   I want to express my gratitude to Professor Jean Paul Brodeur, Director, International Centre for Comparative Criminology (CICC), University of Montreal, for his most valuable and enlightening remarks on this chapter.

2   Laqueur, Walter, 'Reflections on Terrorism' in Charles W. Kegley Jr. and Eugene R. Wittkopf, *The Global Agenda: Issues and Perspectives*, 2nd Edn, New York: Random House, 1988, p. 103.

3   Hocking, Jenny, 'Orthodox Theories of "Terrorism": The Power of Politicised Terminology', *Politics*, 19(2), November 1984, p. 108.

4   For an exhaustive list of contributions to the topic of terrorism in general and its relation to democracy in particular, see *Contre-Terrorisms. Bibliographie. Rapport pour specialistes*, Bruce Beanlands and James Deacon (eds), No. 1988–14, Soliciteur general Canada, Secretariat du Ministère. It is essential to reiterate clearly that our concern with terrorism in the present study is limited to western democracies and to the type of 'individual', 'private', 'group', 'political' and 'state-sponsored' terrorism only. It does not discuss state terror, so often also referred to in the literature under the label of terrorism and describing state, authorities' and governmental violations of human rights and rights of peoples by violent means within the domestic arena. Nor does it deal with foreign policy activities falling within the category of covert actions, foreign support of guerrilla warfare, espionage, etc.

5   To avoid misunderstanding I prefer to use anti-terrorism to stand for governmental policies to control terrorism and to social responses to terrorism. Counter-terrorism has too often been applied to describe governmental abuse of power by applying terrorist methods against terrorists or terrorist-legitimizing populations.

6   Laqueur, *op. cit.*, p. 108.

7   Edwin R.A. Seligman (ed.), 'Intolerance', *Encyclopedia of the Social Sciences*, Vol. 7 New York: Macmillan, 1959, p. 242.

8   Laqueur, *op. cit.*, pp. 103–4.

9   We consciously avoid repeating here the endless discussions relating to the morality of terrorism. See, David C. Rapoport and Yonah Alexander, (eds.) *The Morality of Terrorism*, New York: Columbia University Press, 1989; for the relationship between terrorism and liberal democracy, see Paul Wilkinson, *Terrorism and the Liberal State*, London: Macmillan, 1977; Noemi Gal-Or, *International Cooperation to Suppress Terrorism*, London: Croom Helm, 1985; and many others. Or for the definition of terrorism, see Walter Laqueur *Terrorism*, London: Weidenfeld & Nicolson, 1977. There is, nevertheless, a very generally common attitude, both tacit and explicit, towards violence in democratic societies (including the question of the monopoly of violence

in this type of society) and it is on this general and vague perception that our comparative study is based.

The subjectivity and relativity of the notion of legitimacy, even in the context of liberal democracy is further elucidated by considering the opposite situation too:

> The state may demand obedience from its citizens (Weber 1964:1045), but at the same time may have to consider the reverse: if the institutions of the state do not succeed in attaining their prescribed goals within the limits of certain accepted rules, a loss of legitimacy of these institutions may result. ... [A] loss of legitimacy of the state, of its institutions or actors, is one of the fundamental conditions conducive to severe forms of political violence, crises, and revolutions. (Ekkart Zimmermann, *Political Violence, Crises and Revolutions: Theories and Research*, Cambridge, Mass.: Schenkman Publishing Co., 1983, p. 11.)

10 Lijphart, Arend, *Democracies*, New Haven: Yale University Press, 1984, pp. 1, 2.

11 Gal-Or *op. cit*, pp. 1–7.

12 See p. 43. Another very interesting essay is Reinhard Kreissl's 'Staat und Terrorismus. Anmerkungen zu den Terrorismusstudien', *Kritische Justiz*, 18(1), 1985, pp. 15–28.

13 Chomsky, Noam, *The Culture of Terrorism*, Boston: South End Press, 1988, p. 256.

14 Without prejudice concerning the various origins of terrorism. It is simply a matter of fact that foreign and imported terrorism in western Europe has overwhelmingly originated in the Middle East. It has been the most visible and spectacular non-indigenous terrorism, sparking great attention as well as requiring decisive response. Consequently, it has also aroused certain expectations concerning counter-terrorism policies and their implementation. See, Gal-Or, Noemi, 'Suppressing Terrorism: Problems of European Israeli Cooperation', in Ilan Greisammer and Joseph H.H. Weiler, (eds) *Europe and Israel: Troubled Neighbours*, Berlin, Walter de Gruyter, 1988, pp. 314–37.

15 See Kreissl, *op. cit.*, p. 25.

16 See Raymond Aron for the interaction between the political body and society, in 'Sociologists and Representative Institutions' (1960), in Dominique Schnapper, (Ed.), *Power, Modernity and Sociology*, Edward Elgar, 1988, p. 189.

17 Gross, Felix, 'Some Sociological Considerations', *Violence in Politics*, The Hague: Mouton, 1972, Ch. 6.

Index